D0048890

PETA – A FEMINIST'S PROBLEM WITH MEN

NATIONAL UNIVERSITY
LIBRARY   SAN DIEGO

IN SEARCH OF A THERAPIST

Series Editors: Michael Jacobs and Moira Walker

PETA – A FEMINIST'S PROBLEM WITH MEN

Edited by Moira Walker

OPEN UNIVERSITY PRESS
Buckingham • Philadelphia

Open University Press
Celtic Court
22 Ballmoor
Buckingham
MK18 1XW

and

1900 Frost Road, Suite 101
Bristol, PA 19007, USA

First Published 1995

Copyright © The Editor and Contributors 1995

All rights reserved. Except for the quotation of short passages for the
purpose of criticism and review, no part of this publication may be
reproduced, stored in a retrieval system, or transmitted, in any form
or by any means, electronic, mechanical, photocopying, recording or
otherwise, without the prior written permission of the publisher or a
licence from the Copyright Licensing Agency Limited. Details of such
licences (for reprographic reproduction) may be obtained from the
Copyright Licensing Agency Ltd of 90 Tottenham Court Road,
London, W1P 9HE.

A catalogue record of this book is available from the British Library

ISBN 0–335–19223–8 (pbk)

Library of Congress Cataloging-in-Publication Data

Peta – a feminist's problem with men / edited by Moira Walker.
    p.   cm. — (In search of a therapist)
  Includes bibliographical references.
  ISBN 0–335–19223–8
  1. Feminist therapy. 2. Multiple psychotherapy. I. Walker,
Moira, 1948– . II. Series.
RC455.4.C6P48   1995
616.88'14—dc20   94–24085
                                                            CIP

Typeset by Graphicraft Typesetters Limited, Hong Kong
Printed in Great Britain by St Edmundsbury Press,
Bury St Edmunds, Suffolk

CONTENTS

THE EDITOR AND CONTRIBUTORS

Jennifer Mackewn is a UKCP-registered psychotherapist who is also an associate teaching member of the Gestalt Psychotherapy Training Institute. She has worked previously in commercial and art publishing, in further education and hospital psychiatric services. She lives and practises in Bath and she is also a trainer and supervisor in several psychotherapy institutes.

Judy Moore currently works as a counsellor at the University of East Anglia, and is principal tutor for the postgraduate diploma in person-centred counselling run by the university's Centre for Counselling Studies. Before becoming a counsellor Judy was a teacher, and she has a PhD in English literature.

John Ormrod is a clinical psychologist based at Leicester General Hospital. After reading psychology and biology at the University of Leicester he worked at St Andrew's Hospital, Northampton, prior to his clinical training at Plymouth Polytechnic. Since 1989, he has worked in Leicester within various community and hospital settings.

John Rowan is a psychotherapist and supervisor in private practice, and also teaches at the Minster Centre. He is a member of UKCP, BAC and AHPP, and a Fellow of the BPS. He has been involved with the anti-sexist men's movement since 1973, and is a member of the collective which produces *Achilles Heel*, the British magazine for anti-sexist men.

Maye Taylor is in practice as a chartered counselling psychologist using a feminist psychodynamic approach, and lectures at Manchester Metropolitan University, specializing in women's mental health.

She is an experienced staff consultant, having for several years worked as Equal Opportunities Training Consultant to the GLC.

Christine Wood practises as an art therapist in Sheffield, with clients of Community Health Sheffield. For eight years she edited *Inscape*, the journal of the British Association of Art Therapists, and in 1984 she helped establish an art therapy training course at Sheffield University, where she continues to teach, specializing in the therapeutic needs of people who have a history of psychosis.

Moira Walker is head of the counselling service at the University of Leicester. She is a psychotherapist and writer with a special interest in working with women and with abuse survivors. She also supervises and trains counsellors and psychotherapists.

And Peta, whose contribution forms the core of this book, has for obvious reasons to remain anonymous, although much of her life story is told in full in these pages.

MICHAEL JACOBS AND MOIRA WALKER

SERIES EDITORS' PREFACE

Take five clients, and for each client take six therapists. How will the therapists, or in one case the supervisors as well, understand and work with the following situations?

Charlie is a 40-year-old secretary to a Trades Union official, married with three children:

> I think of myself as someone who lacks self-confidence and feels she always has to apologize for herself, and I'm very insecure. The mildest row with my husband and I think he's going to leave me, and he finds that very irritating, I think. Understandably. I would. Having thought about it, I blame my mother for that. I use the word 'blame' quite consciously, because all the while I very much got the impression when I was young that she didn't love me and doesn't love me. I think of myself as unlovable.

Jitendra is a male Indian psychiatrist, separated from his Irish wife:

> One thing that . . . interests me and sometimes worries me is my early years, my childhood years. I have very few memories of anything before the age of six or five, but I am sure that they have left some legacy behind, a significant legacy, and sometimes I have deep feelings of sadness or complexity or ambivalence which are not immediately ascribable to events happening around me. And I wonder what these . . . what this augurs? I think a therapist might . . . help me in this area. The other area that I am wanting to understand is the dynamics of a large extended family . . . I would like to understand a little bit more about what affects a person's growing up in that context.

Morag is an accountant, the director of a catering business, a mother, stepmother and partner:

> I feel that James wants me to be in the house, to be there because his children are there, and the family's there. He's quite happy to go off and play rugby on Sunday but he likes me being there, being mother-hen . . . I get quite cross, that he keeps trying to push me into the traditional role. I don't feel I've got on as far as I could have done had I been a man, because I had to work twice as hard as everybody else to get where I got, . . . I feel OK always wanting to do something, but it does seem to cause quite a lot of conflict in my life. I feel, 'Is it right that I should always be wanting something new to go at, some new challenge? Should I just be accepting the way I am?'

Peta is an unemployed art teacher living in London:

> I've got a problem with men. At least that's the way that I conceptualize it for the moment. I don't know whether it's a problem with other things as well, but over the last few weeks, particularly – which is a different thing from deep background, I suppose you'd say – some issues seem to have come into my mind that are to do with the fact that I am a woman and they men . . . It's rather difficult to know where to start, except that I feel very self-conscious and rather uncomfortable about the fact that I must also tell you that I'm a feminist. And also that my father was emotionally very distant.

Ruth was abused as a young girl. She wants to hold her male therapist. What can he say when she says to him:

> Your reaction was – or I perceived it as being – a stand-off, and be cold to it, and not let anything happen, which obviously I understand; but I think it just highlighted that my desire . . . is not going to be matched by anyone else's. How can I communicate where I'm at, and help somebody else to understand that, and not necessarily to capitulate to me but just to be understanding?

This unique series of books takes a client's story, his or her presenting difficulties, the current situation, and some of the history from an initial session, recorded verbatim and printed in full for the reader to use. The session has in each case been presented to six different therapists. They address their questions to the client, and explain in each book how they understand the client, how they want to work with the client, what further information they requested, and in the light of what they know, how they forecast the course of therapy. The reader is presented with six possible interpretations and working methods to compare and contrast, with a final telling response from the client and the editor on each of the six therapists.

This series takes a further step forward from the comparative approaches of Rogers and others on film, or the shorter case vignettes in the *British Journal of Psychotherapy*, which have both been deservedly so popular with students and practitioners alike. All the therapists start with precisely the same information, which comes from a largely non-directed initial hour with four real clients. The reader can see in detail how each therapist takes it from there. How they share similar and contrasting insights and interpretations of the same person proves a remarkable and fascinating study of how different therapists work.

The final volume in the series goes a step further and submits one session of the editor's work with a long-term client to six different supervisors. How do they interpret the verbatim material? What questions do they want to ask the therapist? How do they advise the therapist to proceed? In this detailed insight into the work of a therapist and supervisors from different orientations, the reader gets an in-depth view of the value of supervision.

The five volumes in the series are entitled *Charlie – An Unwanted Child?*, *Peta – A Feminist's Problem with Men*, *Morag – Myself or Motherhen?*, *Jitendra – Lost Connections* and, finally, *In Search of Supervision*.

In this particular volume every effort has been made to trace all copyright holders of the poetry quoted in the section on art therapy, if any have been inadvertently overlooked the publisher will be pleased to make the necessary arrangements at the first possible opportunity.

1 THE EDITORS

IN SEARCH OF THE CLIENT

Just how different is the approach used by a therapist from one particular training society from that of a therapist from another orientation? In recent years, there has been much more interest in comparing approaches than in competing approaches. It is sometimes suggested that different methods may suit different clients, or even that therapists tend to select out the clients they can best work with.

There have been other attempts to demonstrate the way in which therapists from different schools might work with the same client. For many years, the two series of short films *Three Approaches to Psychotherapy*, the first made with Rogers, Perls and Ellis and the client 'Gloria', and the second with Rogers, Shostrom and Lazarus and the client 'Kathy', were well used in counselling training. Raymond Corsini tried a similar comparison in print, in the book *Five Therapists and a Client* (F.E. Peacock Publishing, IL,1991), although in our opinion his book is marred by several weaknesses. In the first place, the client is a fictional case, and the first session therefore written entirely from Corsini's imagination – drawing presumably on clients he has known. Second, there are inconsistencies even within the first session, making the case less plausible. Third, each of the responding therapists is asked to imagine how the therapy would go, similarly writing their own dialogue. This gives them *carte blanche* to develop the case along the lines they want their therapy to pursue, which demonstrates the validity of their approach, and in each case ends up with success for their method with the client.

We wanted to approach the question of how different therapists might work with the same client from yet another angle. We wanted a real client, not a fictional situation as in Corsini's work, but more perhaps as Gloria and Kathy were in the sessions recorded with

Rogers and other therapists. In this series, we wanted to preserve the anonymity of the client, which a video or film cannot do. We also wanted to avoid what we believe inevitably happened in *Three Approaches to Psychotherapy*. The client is seen by three therapists in turn, but may be influenced in her responses to the second and third by what has happened in previous interview(s). We wanted all the therapists to start with precisely the same information, and to see how they might take it from there. In this introduction, we explain how we went about that and subsequent parts of the task.

Finding the clients

We used various contacts throughout the country to identify potential participants in the project, providing an outline of the method to be used. We invited applications from people who had never been in therapy before, since we wanted to avoid the contamination of their material by what might otherwise have been influenced from a previous therapist's interpretations. As it turned out, we learned rather late in the day that one of the clients had had a very short period of counselling with a person-centred counsellor, but over a rather different presenting issue to the one she brought to her first session with us.

After meeting those who were interested, and explaining to them the method and the safety features which we describe in more detail below, we invited them to return a consent form if they wished to continue. Their consent did not bind them to take part, until the point at which they finally agreed to release the material that had been taped in the first session. They could withdraw at any moment up to that point at which the therapists would receive their material, and were therefore committed to work on it. We, for our part, promised absolute confidentiality and anonymity (not even the publishers would know their names and addresses), and control by the clients over any material which could lead to identification. We also asked the clients to accept that we could not take them on for therapy, and that we could not be held responsible for their therapy, although we would endeavour to find them the most appropriate therapy if, during the course of our contact with them throughout the project, they so desired it. We also made it clear that we might not use their material, since we would be seeing more people than the series could use.

Several potential candidates dropped out at this stage. Seven people responded that they wished to participate, and between us we arranged to meet those who agreed to take part for an initial interview. We arranged to meet for up to an hour, recording the interviews. We told them as we started that we would say very little, except to prompt them to say a little more where we felt they might value such a response. Some were more fluent than others, but we hope that we did not over-influence the course of the interviews. It was to be the client's agenda which each presented to us, and through us, to their six therapists. Our own interventions are recorded word for word in the record of the first session.

Of the seven interviews, three proved unsuitable for use in the project. All three were as interesting as those we finally chose, but two of them proved too similar as presenting issues to another which we already hoped to use. The third interview concerned us both because of the age of the client, and also because our understanding of the material concerned us. We felt it wiser to leave the client with natural defences. We had to be as sure as we could be from one non-directed interview that our client would survive any of the stresses that might arise in the course of such a project.

We ended up with four tapes from which to work, and we checked with the four clients that they still wanted to proceed before we transcribed the tapes. The second chapter of each volume in the series is a word-for-word transcript of the first interview. The only changes that have been made are to certain possible identifying features. These have been altered with the agreement and with the assistance of the client. The alterations made were internally consistent with the client's presenting story.

Once the transcript was prepared, it was sent to the client to be checked, particularly with regard to any further alterations necessary to disguise actual identity. We did not allow the client to change his or her mind about what had been said, unless to facilitate a disguise of identity, or where there was a clear typing error. Once more we made it clear that the client could withdraw from the project if he or she wished to. Only if the client was completely satisfied with the account to be sent to the therapists, and which would form the key chapter of the book, was the client then asked to assign the copyright of the material to the editors.

Finding therapists

Simultaneously, we started to look for therapists who could represent, at least in their theoretical position, the different approaches we wished to include in each volume. We wanted to find distinct methods or schools for each client, and where possible to have three male and three female therapists. Taking the first four books in the series together, we hoped to represent every major school of therapy. Suggestions were gathered from our own contacts, and therapists who were unable to accept an invitation were asked to suggest a colleague who might. In some cases we asked a professional society to nominate one of its members.

For the most part our task went smoothly enough, and the response we had was encouraging. Many of those who accepted our invitation quite rightly had one major reservation, that their work with clients depended partly (or in some cases largely) upon the face-to-face relationship, and working with its nuances. They accepted that in this case it was impossible to have that particularly subjective experience informing their work, although some more directly than others asked for our own observations, feelings and intuition in some of the questions they asked of us. This concern – a lack of direct contact with the client – was also given as the reason why some of those we approached to represent psychoanalytic psychotherapy turned down our invitation. This was the most difficult space to fill, although other reasons were also given, each one genuine in its own way. We began to wonder whether there was some resistance from therapists in this orientation to 'going public'. But perhaps it was pure coincidence that we had no such problems with any of the other therapies, including other psychodynamic approaches. We occasionally had a refusal, but nearly always with the suggestion of someone else we might ask, who then accepted.

Responding to the client

Our therapists were told, in the original invitation, that having read the material they would have the opportunity to ask further questions of the client, through us the editors. We felt that it would be disruptive for the client to meet each of the six therapists in turn, and that it would make the chances of identification rather greater, since it has remained the case that only the editors know who the clients really are. We were also concerned that we should continue to monitor what was happening for the client in the whole process. This is a person's life and story that we all have responsibility for, and while we wished the therapists to be totally honest, we also wished to ensure the clients survived, without unnecessary damage to them.

The therapists were therefore invited to ask for the further information in order to address the headings we had suggested to them for their chapters to be consistent with one another. We all recognized, on both sides, that therapists would not bluntly ask questions of a client, but that some would take a life history early on, while others would expect such information to emerge during the course of therapy. We had to assume that there was certain information each therapist would hope to receive before the end of therapy. We were unprepared for just how much the therapists wanted to ask, and what we had thought would be a simple second interview proved to be more arduous and searching than either we or the clients could have imagined.

Most of the therapists sent long lists of areas they wished to explore further. Some sent questionnaires or psychometric tests. They asked in some cases for drawings, or for our own personal responses to the client. We were both involved in the Social Atom Exercise in Morag's case, one as director, the other as recorder. We collated the sets of questions so that they could be asked in a more or less natural sequence, putting questions from different therapists about particular aspects of the client's life or history in the same section of the interview, or where they were nearly identical asking them together. Although the therapists only received back the information for which they had clearly asked, where questions were almost the same, they received the same material and a reprint of the other therapist's question. Similar areas were addressed, but very few questions were actually close enough to be asked together. In a few instances, where the client referred back to an answer already given to one therapist, we supplied that information as necessary to a second therapist whose question had evoked this reference.

The interviews with our clients at this stage took several hours – we met at least twice, and in two cases three times. We carefully monitored how much each client could take, and asked periodically how much more he or she wanted to answer in that session. The questions were often searching and they sometimes gave rise to painful feelings and uncomfortable memories, although our experience was that none of the clients found this anti-therapeutic. They and we were stretched more than we might have anticipated, and we valued the immense thoughtfulness which the therapists had put into their questions, and the clients put into their answers.

Inevitably, there was a long gap between the first interview and this subsequent series of separate interviews, which took place much closer together. The original problems may have shifted a little, sometimes being slightly less troubling, sometimes slightly more so. The time lapse did not otherwise have much significance, except in the thought which each client had given to his or her own original material in the intervening period. Their own silent working on this material probably made their responses to the questions rather more full. Certainly many thousands of words were transcribed in each case, once again for the agreement of the client, before being sent off to the individual therapists. In all but one instance, the client was seen by the same person throughout. In Morag's case, her original interview was with Michael. To share the task of editing the four client volumes, it was necessary for her to be allocated to Moira for the second and subsequent interviews and collation of material, although, as already indicated, it rounded the second set of interviews off well for both to be involved in her Social Atom Exercise.

The therapists' task

The therapists' brief was to use the original material and supplementary information which they received from their questions and other 'tests' or questionnaires, to write an assessment of the client along the following lines, which form the main headings of each chapter.

1 A brief description of their own training background, and their therapeutic approach. Even though they are known to represent particular orientations (e.g. person-centred), we recognize that each therapist has particular ways of working, which might draw upon aspects of other approaches. What is important is to see how an actual therapist rather than a theoretical therapy works in practice.

2 The second section consists of the further questions which the therapist asked of the client through the editor therapist, and the responses they feel are relevant to their understanding of the client. Phrases such as 'When I met the client' refer to meeting the client via the editor. For reasons that have been explained already, none of the therapists made contact with or spoke directly to the clients.

3 The therapist's assessment of and reaction to the client – how he or she understands the client and the material the client has presented. This takes different forms, in line with the particular therapeutic approach, empathic identification with the client, counter-transference towards the client, etc. The therapists have been asked to provide indications or evidence of how they arrived at any formulation they might make, even if it is inevitably somewhat speculative.

4 The next section outlines therapeutic possibilities – indications and contra-indications in the client and in the therapist/therapy, in that it may or may not be helpful for that particular client.

5 The fifth section hypothesizes the course of therapy – what form it might take, the methods, the contract, the theoretical approach in practice, and any shifts in approach that might be necessary to accommodate the particular client.

6 Next the therapist suggests possible problem areas and how they might be resolved. We have asked that potential difficulties are faced and not given a favourable gloss if it seems the client might not prove amenable to some aspects of a particular approach.

7 The therapist was asked to explain his or her criteria for success in this case and to try to predict how far these may be met. Aware of the positive outcome in all Corsini's therapists' accounts, we asked the therapists not to predict a totally positive outcome if they had any doubts about it.

8 Each therapist concludes with a short summary and a short reading list for those interested in pursuing his or her approach.

The final stage

As the therapists returned their assessments of the client, and their accounts of how they would work with him or her, these were passed over to the client to read. When all six assessments and accounts had been received, we met with the client for a penultimate session, to discuss the content of the final chapter together, before the editor wrote it. While it had been generally obvious throughout just how much the clients had gained from the process, their own final assessment both of the therapists and of the process is therefore available at the end of each book. We intend to meet with them one more time, when the book is published, to complete our part in their own search for change and understanding.

To them and to the therapists who took part we owe a great debt. They have each in their own way demonstrated a deep commitment to each other, and have furnished the reader with a unique opportunity of comparing not only their own approaches, but also the reader's response to the client with their own. (Following the client's original story in Chapter 2, the reader will find space in Chapter 3 to record ideas, questions and feelings with headings that are similar to those questions we asked each therapist.) The therapists have also shown a willingness to work co-operatively in a project which will do much to advance the comparative study of the many different approaches and nuances which the psychotherapy and counselling world embraces. This series shows how little need there is for competition, and how the different therapies can complement one another in the service of those who seek their help.

2 PETA

A FEMINIST'S PROBLEM WITH MEN

Peta came up to see me from London, where she had heard of our work. She is in her forties. Her near-white hair is swept back close to her head. She is slim and of medium height. She looks serious, and her black-rimmed glasses add to this appearance. She is dressed in dark clothes. Before her sense of humour and thoughtfulness become apparent, she might even be thought to be a little severe. She speaks slowly, at times very slowly, and quite deliberately; but sometimes in a rush, her voice dropping and her words difficult to catch. Her enunciation is polished, her words sometimes stressed with feeling, although the feeling has a slightly forced quality to it. She has notes in her hand, to which she refers, and I have no need to prompt her or to encourage her further until the point, as it becomes clear, when she has worked through her notes. It then feels as if Peta finds it difficult to know what more to say in the session.

I've got a problem with men. At least that's the way that I concep-tualize it for the moment. I don't know whether it's a problem with other things as well, but over the last few weeks, particularly – which is a different thing from deep background, I suppose you'd say – some issues seem to have come into my mind that are to do with the fact that I am a woman and they men.

And . . . it's rather difficult to know where to start, except that I feel very self-conscious and rather uncomfortable about the fact that I must also tell you that I'm a feminist. And also that my father was emotionally very distant. So . . . we have a situation where I know that to be angry about men in general is . . . actually for a person such as myself who's involved in counselling, not very helpful. It spreads the net too wide and it also represents a certain amount of projected anger, and so on, and so on.

Now I trace backwards in time to the kind of person my father was; and forwards to when I was seventeen and eighteen, which was an extremely troubled time for me – later adolescence or mid-adolescence, a time of crisis; through my twenties when my father died, and there wasn't any longer a chance to grow into another kind of relationship with him; the reasons why I got married, and the reasons why the marriage relationship went through the phases that it did, which were critical, I feel, a series of crises. My son was born fifteen years ago, and I am the primary parent. I was divorced ten years ago, and have had a series of relationships with men who . . . those relationships have been rather unstable, transient. For long months of the year, for many months of the year, I am quite celibate and really rather content with that.

I am generally speaking a happy and contented individual who has much joy – I have much joy in my life. I left full-time teaching three years ago. I'm among other things an art teacher, and came to counselling via an interest in art therapy – art therapy is only available at certain centres in the country so I'm told – I was drawn in by doing an introductory art therapy course.

Quite recently, when I was doing my homework, and writing essays is a daunting task, I found that 5000 words is quite a lot – I was sweating over the essay, reading, writing and thinking, and putting together ideas. So when I knew I had this interview with you I put myself in the middle of a sort of spider diagram. And the prongs out . . . I've actually done five blobs, coming out of the middle that happens to be me.

And the first one . . . I should start at the top left-hand corner – it makes me smile, and it would make my course tutor smile. I have problems with authority figures, and I've written down this clump of ideas, this area of 'authority figures' [it's headed]: public life, career, the interview as arena, subverting the facilitator. I learned some of those things by direct feedback as a result of training in counselling. I know I do it. Sometimes it causes me great pain . . . the consciousness. I do not now apply for any jobs, although probably the thing I want most for myself is a career. And I gave up looking for full-time work about . . . maybe I never have, since leaving teaching, because I would rather face difficulties of doing without a career than face the feeling of being rejected. I think it's got something to do with my – maybe some people wouldn't accept this, but I describe it, I conceptualize it by saying: I think it's got something to do with my conditioning as a woman. I do not want to compete in that way and it is painful to me to have to accept that actually [*and here Peta moves on without a breath to the next point*] . . .

The second clump here, I move on the spider diagram and move round clockwise, I've headed 'Brian', who is my ex-husband, the father of my son, who actually I have really quite a good relationship with: distant, but good, warm. The history of our relationship has violence implied or direct attached to it. Although I've never been a battered wife, there's been a lot of implied violence within the relationship. He collected guns. I experienced his withdrawal as using silence as a weapon, and felt deserted, very strongly. I can go back into that time if necessary, it's part of my own biography, and there's quite a lot of pain attached to some of that stuff but [*and again Peta does not pause*] I'll move on to the third little clutch of ideas . . .

. . . which is headed 'Kevin', who's my brother. He's nine years younger than myself and the only family that I have is really my mother and my brother. My mother lives in Bristol and my brother lives in Carlisle – geographically quite distant, and I feel that very much because I'm a single parent, and as a woman that's important. Kevin's training to be a community worker. There is much material that is not dealt with between us. Sometimes the consciousness of that is really very difficult to bear. I saw him a few weeks ago – he was not talking really at all. He was not making a big issue of it, but I knew that free communication was not possible at this visit. He stayed for a week. [*Peta clears her throat twice.*] There have been past power struggles between us: a gap of nine years with siblings is difficult. There are . . . the history of my relationship with my brother includes my father and – I kind of run out of words because it gets a bit deeper at that point – and what I'll do is move round to the last two sections. I can go back . . . I can go in . . .

The fourth section on the diagram here is my father, who was ten years older than my mother, and it would be proper to describe their relationship as . . . their marriage relationship was difficult, and strained. And I think now, looking back as an adult along with the problems I had as a child were not only – well I'm reluctant to blame, but when I think of the relationship between my parents it's difficult to get into that feeling without saying 'You screwed up . . .', basically. I was an extremely isolated child, who was bullied at school, hated school, was extremely withdrawn, took refuge in books, had no close friends except for one other girl. I lived on a houseboat; it was a converted boat; and my father worked abroad, so my mother raised me. My father came back periodically – it wasn't continuous. My mother is the daughter of a well-to-do solicitor in Chelmsford further inland – was then, but our situation was not reflected . . . we lived on a houseboat in a creek, and so the class values – if you like, although I'm suspicious of that description – were not reflected in my environment. So I was brought up with a middle-class accent by a woman who happened to have a middle-class accent. But I was put into a school that was not like that. And I was *profoundly* bored and bullied by both teachers and kids really. And so I turned off. I withdrew.

It was unsafe too for children to go down to the water. The kids didn't go down to the creek. It was not the place kids played. It was the only place I could play . . . one of the places I did play was my father's workshop – because it was basically the only place apart from the quay itself. I had my own cabin which was in the fo'c'sle – I've pictures of it still: I had all my books lined up, great beams, and that sort of thing. My father was an engineer, a carpenter and joiner and fitter, and a practical man who *did* things. So his workshop was equipped with all kinds of interesting materials. Anyway, I don't know . . . I remember distinctly a feeling, a great rising sense, of sickness, of isolation that he *didn't know how* to communicate to me, a kind of *boredom*. If you're bored as a kid it can be experienced physically. And sometimes children – I use entirely my own experience here – sometimes children experience distress physically; it's very odd this, I'm learning a lot really from this conversation. [*She sighs*.] Oh!

The last section on the diagram is headed 'lovers'. [*Peta pauses*.] I have in the past made quite disastrous . . . what turned out to be unwise . . . and recently I thought I'd got it sussed. I smile, a sardonic smile. [*She pauses*.] A man I know suggested that we sort of get it together, and he turned out to be rather an inappropriate person. I think I was . . . I think I was . . . I'm ashamed to say I think I was flattered by the attention. I shouldn't have been really, in the sense that I get a lot of love from friends, and the work I do. And I actually didn't even at any stage get very much from him, because he turned out [*again she pauses*] to be really quite damaging. I pulled away and pulled out and withdrew before deep damage could be done. At least I have that kind of sense. [*There is another pause*.] But I realized that he was another *man*; I realized that it was not going to be possible; I realized that the way that I am with men is a complicated business, and it goes backwards and forwards and it's got a middle and it's got a sort a shape to it, and this business it just won't go away and I want to deal with it.

This recent man friend, ex-friend, was a very angry person it turned out. So I'm looking – this is hindsight – he used silence as a weapon. And I bring this cluster of ideas to the tape and to you, because I don't . . . I want to be a good counsellor, I don't want to be the kind of – nothing will shake me from my feminist convictions. I have a spiritual commitment to feminism, it's a sort of profound thing for me, and has grown and changed with me over the years. So it isn't that I have doubts in that specific kind of way, but I know that if I'm going to be a good counsellor I'm going to have to deal with this. I want to be a good parent for my adolescent son. I think I am actually. Most of the time. I think we have found that. I want to be a decent sister to my brother, because we're such a small family and it pains me that so much . . . stuff . . . I mean he's sensitive and intelligent and he's going to work with people, and he knows the value of good communication, and respects the healing work that people can do. I don't particularly want to find a man for a lover, because I'm not interested in being married, in the conventional sense. I want to be able to handle my own sexuality in my own kind of way, which I actually think I do, and yet I don't – obviously.

I wrote down under the diagram some little bits and pieces that were coming into my head. 'Mothers get blamed'. I feel very difficult about that. Some of the gender stuff simply won't go away. I've tried to raise the general issue of gender issues in counselling with my tutors – unsuccessfully. They are either threatened, or they simply choose not to deal with it. So obviously the best place to do this is in either supervision or in my own therapy. It's why I bring it here.

If I sense that someone is afraid of me, which they sometimes are – I am . . . I can be threatening. I will withdraw. If I sense that a person is unable to look at gender issues, or there is tension around that, then I will withdraw, because it's not genuine; and it doesn't feel right or comfortable; or I'm making matters worse. 'She's just a crazy feminist, you can't talk to her' – you know. Or if I do manage to engage at all I get, 'It doesn't matter whether you are a man or a woman', which I think is displacing. I could be wrong. So I'm very interested in all this.

I have a sense that the deep past does have a profound influence on what I'm walking round in, in the present. And I've written down here: 'I know that my mother and brother had a close relationship'; and my mother actually admits her Oedipus Schmoedipus – half our family is Jewish – and she laughs about it. But I know she's not laughing about it either – she adores him, it's wonderful, it's good! But I had no coalition with my father. I . . . my mother told me that my father adored me. [*She says very quietly and quickly.*] That's not the same thing. [*Her voice goes back to a normal level.*] When I was growing up I guess I loved him. I hated him for dying, sure as hell, I was very angry, and that's probably part of it too. And now I have no coalition with my brother and I *need* that in my relationship with my mother, because my mother is very strong-willed. She . . . she's neurotic in some ways, although I am reluctant to throw that kind of label about. She's a very intelligent woman, and quite learned in her own way. There was a time when I could not bear to be near her, and a lot of my life I actually spent being very afraid of my mother. Adolescence was horrendous: I ran away from home. I was into – this was the early sixties – I was . . . I was . . . for a whole year I took acid once a week. It was freely available in the sort of sub-culture kind of way at that time, and if you were a beatnik or a person of that kind it was . . . it was available. It was a crazy time, that time. There's more around that stuff. When I needed coalitions and equality, there was nothing. [*Peta's voice drops right down.*] I think I am *very angry* about that now [*her voice returns to a normal level*] and I'm intrigued by this gender . . . what I call, gender agenda.

It won't go away. There isn't anything I can do. I want to make sense of it. I am *pursued* by the necessity to make sense of it. In the training that I am doing as a counsellor, I have been told . . . the feedback I get is that I have . . . that I do subvert facilitators. And by Christ I'm sure I do. I do. I know I do. And I don't just subvert men. I subvert facilitators because they're authority figures. I subverted a tutor – sounds awful [*she laughs*] 'I subverted a tutor' – who was leading an art therapy course because she was making various psychodynamic interventions in personal territory that I found deeply, deeply threatening, and I withdrew. But that's experienced as a weapon, not as an inept therapist, which is actually, in my professional capacity, I believe it to be the case. She misjudged some of the issues. I . . . I don't know . . .

[*She pauses.*] Where am I? Stop the tape. [*She laughs, a little nervously.*] Prompt me or . . . or interrupt.

[*I say that I do not want to lead her in any direction, but it feels as if she has got to the end of what she has prepared. Peta laughs. I say it is hard for her to know what to do with it, but I encourage her to take it anywhere she'd like to. I say that she has clearly thought about it a lot, and that if it feels right to draw it to a close . . .*]

No! No! I don't know. We'll go on. Ten minutes?

[*I say, 'As long as you like, we have an hour. But whatever feels right'.*] Let's work for another fifteen. [*I say, 'Whatever feels right to you'.*]

I *have* thought about it a lot. I've thought about it a great deal, and I have a kind of sense that thinking [*she whispers*] doesn't always get places. [*She pauses.*] Because I've given some of these matters great thought, and because I spend long periods alone, I'm relatively self-sufficient. I do a lot of good work. The company of myself is as much as I need. I depend upon people but I am also dependent upon being alone. But I'm finding that this material doesn't move. There's a circularity of some of the thinking. My brother leaves to go back to Carlisle and I'm thinking, I'm bumbling round the garden, weeding, thinking, 'We didn't even talk to each other. He stayed for five or six days. Now what am I going to do with this?'

We don't have to spend our lives in deeply serious committed intellectual discourse, but he didn't actually speak to me at all. About anything. He didn't ask me and I couldn't ... And when we were in the company of some very good friends of mine in the next street, he talked to the *man*. All four of us went, my son, and my mum and my brother, and visited Judy and Hal – and they have three kids, so it was a happy time, kind of fluid social set-up. Because Hal knows me very well, he's able to take one or two risks. And I with him. I like Hal. He said – Hal was sitting down, and my brother was sitting down, and I was kind of going out the door – Hal said, 'You love your brother, don't you?' with great confidence. And then because Hal's a very sensitive man, he intuitively picked up in my response – and he threw out the remark perfectly innocently – but instantaneously he knew that within me I had been thinking, 'What ... ? Why ... does he come? What am I going to do? I can't talk to the guy'. And then immediately without me saying a thing Hal said, 'Ah, you *sometimes* love him'; and then because I didn't say anything – he was sitting here, right ... you know – he said, 'Well, you *like* him then ... '; and he kind of decelerated, which was ... I mean, it was OK and I'm not in any way angry about it. But it was such an obvious thing, and there wasn't a thing I could do. All I did was just stand there. I couldn't ... It was like somebody'd just put up a mirror, a full-length brightly lit mirror, and there it was staring us both in the face really. I'm afraid of my brother. I think. I am afraid of what men represent. And sometimes I'm afraid of men because I feel they can, they have more power.

Now, because I'm rather widely read on certain aspects of feminism I can be drawn into a kind of sociopolitical analysis, of why I feel threatened by men, because they represent power. And I can dissemble patriarchy if I'm called upon to do so; but that ... I think ... I don't know ... I think that the question ... I want to move on the thing, I'm getting *tired* of being turned away from, so I'm actually getting angry, and I realize that when I'm faced with silence, or with a low-key emotional response, the blank screen in therapy, I find it not only threatening but traumatizing because of the history of ... [*Peta pauses.*] And sometimes I feel very low in my spirits about the fact that I'm not able to feel comfortable with men as friends. There is always a sexual element, because I am a sexual being. I have had gay relationships in the past but the stage of life I am in at the moment I am apparently heterosexual – I don't mean to be flippant about this. And I would like to be comfortable with men, as equals. And sometimes I want that so much I say, 'Give it to me. Give me equality. [*Peta raises her voice.*] I demand it!' – which of course isn't really, isn't really the way to do things. I can't sweep away my political consciousness, that we live in a deeply, *deeply* patriarchal society. So that everywhere I look . . . I mean if you wrote an unpatriarchalized Bible you'd have a pamphlet. If you put as many women as there are men in parliament you would transform the country. But I'm not saying that women are any better, particularly in politics maybe. It remains to be seen. Well, we have Maggie Thatcher to . . . [*she smiles*] no more needs to be said!

I would like to move . . . I think . . . I think, yes, where can I take it? I get . . . it pains me that men I respect turn away from me so soon. Because they feel disempowered. I mean Ed, or Hamish, a man whom I love to be around, I like listening to him, I learn things from him, I not only enjoy his company, but I respect his teaching, and the way he conducts himself, and Ed – as it happens Ed and Hamish are my tutors; but I want more from them. And it's not comfortable to want more at a deeper level. Hamish [*she pauses slightly*] is easily . . . threatened really. It's not a secure thing for him, he feels cut off at the knees, emasculated, so I . . . because I . . . it's easy for me to feel close to him in a therapeutic sense. I . . . OK, that's for now. I won't touch that . . .

Ed stonewalls. I know that among my peer group on the counselling course I'm either a pain in the arse because I've got a lot to say for myself, or I'm OK because I listen and I'm good. And I know I'm good. I'm seen as confident because that's how I come across. Kurt Vonnegut said we have to be careful how we seem to be; and I am. And I'm learning more and more how to be careful because I don't actually want to be seen as confident. It doesn't actually match . . . congruence.

I think that's . . . actually it would be nice to feel congruent with men in a more general sense; and specifically, the deep history. I remember – I'm grass-hopping – my father and brother used to play-fight on the floor, like kids and parents do. I do still with my own son thank God, except he's triumphant. I don't mind. But that was really difficult: here was I, and my brother was play-fighting with my father. He was five, let's say, and I was at a stage, nine years older [*she speaks very slowly*], when I needed something, I certainly needed attention [*there is a long pause*], which I never got. And the *unspeakable* fury of deprivation still assails me sometimes. I have to be very careful how I remember that. And so, if I . . . I want to reclaim any part, at least some part of my relationship with my brother, because he's going to be all there is. Because you know my mother's nearly seventy.

I might be a better woman, parent for my son, who deserves the best. So maybe I can . . . [*she laughs*] Cut. That's it!

THE READER'S

RESPONSE

Before reading further, the reader is given space to record a personal response to the client, and to questions similar to those which the six therapists were asked to address.

What does this client make you feel?

How might you use what you feel in understanding and working with this client?

What more do you want to know? Is there any information which is crucial at this stage?

Thus far, how do you understand this client and the material she has presented?

What indications are there so far in this client that lead you to feel that you could work with her?

What contra-indications are there?

What, if any, will be your focus?

What will be your method, as related to this client?

What difficulties do you anticipate you might encounter?

What in your view might be a favourable outcome for this client?

JENNIFER MACKEWN

GESTALT PSYCHOTHERAPY

The therapist

I underwent extensive training in a range of humanistic approaches in counselling and psychotherapy, including creative therapies such as art therapy, psychodrama and various forms of body work. I then specialized in Gestalt psychotherapy. I am a UKCP-registered psychotherapist, as well as a Teaching Member of the Gestalt Psychotherapy Training Institute. I have done further post-registration training in integrative psychotherapy. I have worked in commercial and art publishing, in further education and in the psychiatric services of several hospitals.

I now work as a psychotherapist and as a trainer and supervisor in several psychotherapy training institutes, as well as writing on psychotherapeutic topics. My immediate interests in the field of psychotherapy vary: they include creativity in psychotherapy and the similarities and differences between Gestalt psychotherapy, Jungian analysis and Object Relations.

I understand Gestalt psychotherapy as a holistic and relational approach that emphasizes the wholeness and integrity of the individual within the context of his or her environment and social, historical and cultural milieu. Gestalt psychotherapy is based in field theory and dialogic relationship. It proposes that the meaning of individuals and of their behaviour can only be understood in terms of the ever-shifting relationship between them, their lifespaces and fellow human beings.

My practice of Gestalt psychotherapy is broad, embracing a comparative knowledge of some psychoanalytic approaches and of several creative and body therapies. In many respects, my comprehensive approach is typical of the best Gestalt. Unfortunately, Gestalt has

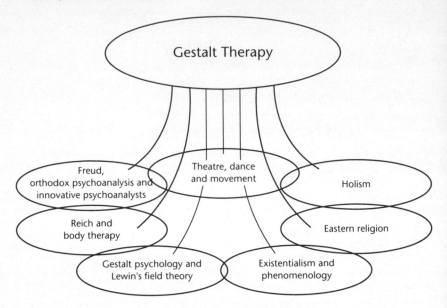

Figure 1 Sources of early Gestalt Therapy

been frequently misrepresented and trivialized, many people believing that it consists of a few dramatic techniques, such as the famous two-chair dialogue. This is a serious misunderstanding.

From its earliest inception in the 1940s, Gestalt psychotherapy was rooted in and drew from a rich heritage, as shown in Fig. 1. In the last two decades, Gestalt theorists have continued to integrate concepts from other approaches and to develop and refine practice and theory. As an eminent Gestalt theorist explains:

> We have always been an integrating framework. That's one of the things I love about Gestalt therapy. We don't have to recreate the wheel. We take what we need from the total field . . . This freedom from dogma is characteristic of Gestalt therapy.
>
> (Yontef 1988: 6)

Further information requested

What does Peta want from psychotherapy?
Through Moira I summarized my understanding of Peta's objectives for therapy: 'You would like to improve your relationships with

men and with "authority figures". More specifically, you "would like to be comfortable with men as equals". You want to deal with gender issues in therapy and you feel that the trainers on your counselling course have felt "threatened" or have ignored you when you have raised them.'

'The language that you use to describe yourself conveys a sense that you lacked contact and relationship at certain key periods in your life. For example, you talk of yourself as "extremely isolated", "caught in the circularity of your own thinking", "needing attention". This leads me to suppose that you may want to explore the themes of relationship and isolation/withdrawal in a broad sense?'

Peta confirmed that I had understood the main things she wanted from therapy, adding that she hoped to come to a place of peaceful restedness regarding the rage she carries, and to be able to pick it up and put it down.

Peta's expectations from psychotherapy

I asked Peta what she imagined were the worst and best things that could result from therapy. The worst thing would be 'to embark on an intimate journey with a therapist and find that they in some way abused that, by the wrong exercise of power, sexual overtones'; and the best would be 'those magical moments . . . when there is a sense of very important communication'.

I suggested to Peta that she visualize leaving therapy some time in the future and describe how she would look, walk, talk, feel or be different? She replied, 'Kind of something that won't appear on the tape for you'. Moira commented: 'This was an alive moment – Peta breathes in deeply, flings her arms wide in a very expansive manner, smiles warmly, sits up straight. My image is that Peta is allowing life in and welcoming it'.

Peta's background and means of support

I explored several aspects of Peta's background and current circumstances to assess whether she has sufficient support in herself and her life to embark upon self-exploration, which can be challenging. No single answer would cause me to decide to take Peta on or refer her elsewhere – it is the whole picture which leads me to make this decision.

The question of whether Peta or members of her family had ever suffered from mental illness or depression met with a hesitant response: 'Not of depression or mental . . . it may be possible to describe my father as perpetually depressed. I have a little difficulty with that question because nobody ever named these things. My mother during my childhood, I'm quite sure, must have been depressed . . . but nobody being admitted to psychiatric hospital and no schizophrenia in the history'.

When I enquired whether Peta had used drugs, including coffee, alcohol and nicotine, she said that she uses cannabis from time to time: 'I have actually in the past over-used cannabis; it blocks, you know, it insulates . . . Nicotine: I'm not too bad. I do drink. I drink just prior to bed. . . . it's to knock me out actually so I don't lie there'.

I asked Peta about her parents and family and how she currently supports herself. She explained that her mother is an important source of support, although she has chronic asthma, bone cancer and is increasingly immobile. Peta recognized it will be very hard to lose her. She talked of being a single parent and of her son, explaining that he had recently separated from her psychologically. She initially experienced this as 'a crisis', coped with by 'ranting' to her mother. She also said her son's need for space has meant that she has deepened her relationship with two men friends.

Peta explained that her father is dead and that her mother has told her that her father adored her; but that she herself cannot experience that love, which contributes to the pain and rage she feels about the loss. Peta twice said her parents 'did not appear to have a relationship'.

When I asked Peta how her family and friends would react if they knew she was contemplating therapy, she said that they already know because she is quite open about it as it is a valid extension of her training.

Will Peta benefit from working with the Gestalt approach?
To gain a sense of Peta's reactions to my ways of working, I made interventions that represent the full range of my style, including the holistic, creative, active and exploratory possibilities of Gestalt. I also explained some aspects of the Gestalt approach.

Peta picked up invitations to visualize very imaginatively and readily, as described above when I asked her to visualize herself leaving therapy some time in the future. She responded to suggestions for creative exploration of things she had described. For example, I asked if she would be willing to draw her and her brother and the 'unspeakable fury of deprivation' that she had experienced when her brother and father had play-fought together. She sat down on the floor and drew the picture shown in Fig. 2 with absorption, commenting on her own process of realization as she did so: 'I didn't think it would turn out like this [*laughs to herself*] . . . the unspeakable fury of deprivation – it isn't my own phrase [*still drawing, speaking quietly*], but it obviously had a lot of impact and still does . . .

[*finishes drawing, sits back and looks at it*]. Phew . . . wow . . . um . . . that's me down in the corner alone'.

My understanding of Gestalt therapy
I explained various aspects of Gestalt therapy via Moira, which produced what felt like a three-way dialogue between Peta, Moira and myself:

> *J.M.:* In your first session, you talked about the therapist being like a blank screen. Well, in Gestalt therapy the therapist does not necessarily try to present a blank screen – we believe that real human relationships are important and potentially healing so sometimes I may ask you questions, reveal my responses or tell you how I am feeling – while at the same time keeping the overall time and process focused on you.
>
> *Peta:* I feel tremendously warmed by that kind of description.

Moira commented that Peta listened very attentively, was clearly interested and looked perhaps a little anxious.

> *J.M.:* I see therapy as a form of equal partnership, in which we both have specialized and different skills and responsibilities. I bring therapeutic tools as well as support and attention. You bring yourself and your expertise on yourself and how you experience the world.
>
> *Peta:* That's telling me something about a kind of equality which is enormously valuable, I think. Yes. And has all kinds of implications, the way that resonates . . . so there's a kind of dignity about that which is enormously appealing.

Moira described Peta as very engaged with my statement and said that her answer was very 'real' – 'she was really there'.

> *J.M.:* I can't do the work of changing you or your life circumstances for you, but I am willing to attend to you, share my reactions with you and reflect on how I experience you.
>
> *Peta:* Now that's pretty concrete. There are parts of me that are terribly vulnerable so I'd wish them to take care of me. (Just tread around the bits that are going to sort of . . . pop up.) I would like that, I would learn very much.

Moira felt that I had really captured Peta's imagination with this statement: 'She is very interested and has good eye contact. The

Figure 2 Peta's spontaneous drawing: 'Unspeakable fury of deprivation'

parentheses denote where it felt to me as if she were speaking through me direct to you: a powerful moment'.

> *J.M.:* I work holistically, which means I attend to and work with all aspects of you and myself – body, mind and spirit . . .
> *Peta:* I wish all aspects of our society would encompass and embrace – what a nice word – those inter-related elements. There would be a great sense of healing for us all . . . it's a very painful split between mind and body . . . we don't discuss spiritual matters very much, it's a secularized thing and there's a lack, a loss . . . Thank you that person.

Moira remarked that Peta's response to all the above points was 'very active and interested. She responds warmly, although some vulnerability and hesitation shows in her eyes. At the last point about your holistic approach she visibly relaxes; she breathes in deeply, as though she is physically allowing your words in. It is as though she softens. She is physically still, warm and receptive and obviously touched deeply. Her last words are really heartfelt and again feel like a direct communication to you'.

Lack of relationship
There is an unrealistic side of this book. The relationship between client and therapist is the crucible which holds the therapy. It is the means of contact and of potential healing. The stages of its development inform all the therapist says or does. I would only ask my questions in the context of that relationship. Yet I am not in relationship to Peta, at least not in the normal sense.

What does Peta need to know about me?
I told Moira that I would be prepared to say something about myself and my professional background and to answer Peta's questions, unless they felt too personal in which case I would say so. Peta responded, 'I appreciate a certain amount of self-disclosure . . . very much and again it just feels more equal'.

I felt alerted to Peta's anxieties regarding therapy and to her realistic awareness of the potential exploitation which has arisen in some therapies. I would explain that I belong to GPTI and BAC and practise by their Code of Ethics, which means I am accountable for the quality of my work, in the same way as members of other professional organizations.

Assessment

Assessment and diagnosis have often been used to objectify the client, treat her more as a case than a person and imply a fixed state. Insensitive and reductionistic diagnostic assessment may be inconsistent with the development of an equal and open partnership and of an 'I–Thou' relationship between therapist and client (Yontef 1980; Hycner 1985; Jacobs 1989).

Key premises in the Gestalt approach include the idea that every individual is a whole, different from and greater than the sum of the individual parts; that the essence of the whole can never be captured by an analysis of the different bits; that the self is not a fixed entity but a constantly changing *process* that evolves and defines itself in relationship to others. To assess Peta in a manner which is consistent with these principles, I attempt to describe and discuss Peta not as a fixed entity but in terms of (1) her *process* of relating to and contacting the world, and (2) her *process* of moderating contact. I then meditate upon the possible meanings of the above processes to Peta's whole person.

Peta's process of making contact

An essential concept is that of contact. There are many facets of the concept of contact which are well described in Gestalt literature (Zinker 1978; Clarkson and Mackewn 1993). For the purposes of this section, the reader needs to be familiar with the following terms:

- *Cycle of contact:* processes by which healthy individuals continually make contact with their environment and withdraw from it, in a natural self-regulatory cycle designed to meet their needs in relationship to those of the human community, as illustrated in Fig. 3.
- *Contact style:* the processes by which individuals moderate their contacting, including desensitization, deflection, introjection, projection, confluence and retroflection. The nature of these different styles of moderating to contact is illustrated by the examples drawn from Peta's ways of moderating her contact.

I start describing Peta's contact/withdrawal cycle from the point of withdrawal:

- *Withdrawal.* Peta describes herself as 'extremely withdrawn' and being 'isolated' in childhood. She 'withdrew' when an art therapy tutor made various psychodynamic interventions that she found 'deeply, deeply threatening'.

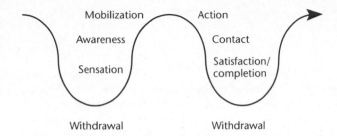

Figure 3 Awareness–excitement–contact cycle. Adapted from Zinker (1978)

- *Sensation.* Peta vividly describes the sensations of unhappiness she experienced as a child: 'I remember distinctly a feeling, a great rising sense, of sickness, of isolation that he [father] didn't know how to communicate to me, a kind of boredom . . . sometimes children experience distress physically'.
- *Awareness.* Peta seems to have a high degree of psychological and intellectual awareness. For example, she realized that she uses a process of withdrawal to defend herself, like others use towards her. She seems aware of a range of emotional reactions, describing many more painful awarenesses than pleasant ones.
- *Mobilization of energy.* Peta mobilized *verbally* for the exchange between herself and Moira, using the support of her notes. She mobilizes more fully and spontaneously in response to my description of Gestalt therapy as an equal partnership or holistic exploration and to my request that she draw herself and her brother.
- *Action.* Peta is active in her garden and house. She has taken action to apply for and attend a counselling course. Yet Peta says that she does not apply for any jobs and has given up looking for work, although what she wants most is a career.
- *Contact.* Peta talks more about withdrawal, isolation, lack of relationship (between her parents), distant relationship, lack of communication, and difficulties with intimacy, than about contact and intimacy. She seems to know the isolation–withdrawal pole of the contact–withdrawal continuum better than the contact–relationship pole.
- *Satisfaction and completion.* Although Peta does not talk specifically about satisfaction, she refers to feelings of contentment: 'I am generally speaking a happy and contented individual who has much joy – I have much joy in my life'. On the other hand, a notable feature of Peta's style or process of communication is that she

often does not complete sentences but lets them drift. I am interested to know what this means to Peta and explore this below.

Peta's process of moderating contact

We all moderate the process of contact awarely and healthily, as our priorities in the evolving circumstances of the field change. Habitual, unaware interruptions to the contact process on the other hand, may maintain fixed patterns of behaviour that deny or displace needs or feelings, which have for some reason in the past been found too problematic. What is interesting from the Gestalt perspective is to consider *how* and *when* Peta interrupts her contacting, and to investigate with her *of what service* it may be (or have been) to her whole self to do so *in that way, at those times*. Below I describe different ways in which Peta moderates her contact process.

- *Desensitization*. Peta has desensitized herself through the use of cannabis and still desensitizes herself through the use of alcohol at night prior to sleeping.
- *Deflection*. Peta deflects by not answering questions directly and by using rather impersonal, theoretical language. She also seems to deflect by inserting a marked number of sub-clauses in each sentence and by not completing her statements.
- *Introjection*. Introjection consists of taking into our system ideas or aspects of the environment from others without assimilation. It is often characterized by the phrases 'I should . . . ' rather than 'I want to . . . '. I am not yet clear how Peta introjects, but she *may* have introjected beliefs that she should not express strong feelings of rage or pain directly, for fear of being too much for others or for herself; and that she needs to be perfect or get things right.
- *Projection*. It seems likely that Peta disowns her own power and projects it on to men and authority figures. As a result she fears them, feels uncomfortable and unequal with them, or resents and subverts them. It is also important to acknowledge and respect Peta's view that the inequality she experiences is not merely due to projection, but has cultural, political and familial reality. There are many ways that men have more power than women; and in her family Peta seems to have been loved differently from her brother.
- *Retroflection*. Although Peta says she feels rage, she does not indicate how she expresses it. Later she says she feels uncomfortable with her rage; so she may hold back (or retroflect) her powerful angry feelings. She seems to have habitually retroflected her fury

towards her brother's and father's playfighting and her blame of her parents.

- *Confluence.* Confluence occurs when two people flow together without a sense of differentiation. In professional settings, Peta may be subtly confluent, when she subverts or withdraws from authority rather than directly confronting it. In personal matters she seems sometimes to be more obviously confluent, for example she does not speak to her brother for five days, partly because he does not speak to her.

Formal assessment

Despite my already expressed reservations, many Gestalt therapists are now trained to use formal diagnostic systems, in order to communicate with members of the wider psychiatric community; to ensure they make professional assessments regarding the appropriateness of psychotherapy for their clients; and to develop tentative therapeutic plans for different clients. The description of manifest characteristics of the individual featured in the *Diagnostic and Statistical Manual of Mental Disorders* (DSM III-R, APA 1987) is reasonably compatible with a phenomenological approach. Its system of five axes (which constitute interacting sub-systems of a whole) is reasonably compatible with field theory and with a view of the self as variable process. Although Peta does not meet the criteria for a diagnosis in terms of the DSM-III-R, her styles of relating as represented in the transcript may show some mildly avoidant and passive aggressive traits.

My responses and relationship to Peta

When I first received the transcript reproduced here on pp. 8–15, I found it hard to concentrate and to get a sense of the person I was trying to meet. Peta's sentences were circumlocutory, leaving me wondering what her statement or conclusion was. Re-reading the transcript, I felt invigorated by Peta's energy for her own beliefs, touched by her courage and increasingly aware of wishing to reach out to that part of her that she still keeps isolated, while taking care not to make her feel invaded. As described, I made statements through Moira directly to Peta and Peta on several occasions responded directly to me. I was surprised to discover that in the course of conceiving this chapter, I did in fact experience a fresh sense of contact and relationship between us as two human beings, despite the distance of time, space, paper and an intermediary. From Moira's observations and Peta's own words, it also seems probable that Peta at times felt in relationship with me. To make the exercise alive, I occasionally fantasized that Peta would in fact come into therapy with me.

Therapeutic possibilities

Indications of success

If Peta decided to come into therapy with me I would take her on, subject to confirming a mutual willingness to work together. She seems to have sufficient self and environmental support to sustain therapy. She has aims for her therapeutic exploration which are reasonably realistic. She seems highly motivated. She has clearly been able to use therapeutic contact (as represented by her talks with Moira and indirectly with the six therapists) to reflect on her own process, to develop her awareness and to work independently in between sessions. She has recognized that thinking things out alone has now become circular. She seems ripe to break that circularity and engage with another person in exploring her own process.

I see strong indications that Peta could use Gestalt therapy with me successfully. She is enormously enlivened by my descriptions of my understanding of therapy, illustrated in her responses to my descriptions of the holistic, person-to-person nature of Gestalt. Further, when I ask Peta for her best expectation of therapy, her reply is close to recent Gestalt expositions of the dialogic relationship, in which the highest moment is the mutual 'I–Thou' meeting: 'The best thing would be those magical moments . . . when there is a sense of very important communication'.

The aim of a Gestalt therapist is not to act as a change agent but to develop the individual's awareness of how she functions, in turn increasing her choices of how she relates to others (Beisser 1970; Yontef 1980). In line with these aims, I believe Peta could develop her awareness of how she currently operates around men and increase her range of relationship tools within a six-month period. She may also begin to establish a sense of the fixed patterns of behaviour which she perpetuates in the present, sabotaging or limiting current relationships.

Contra-indications

Six months may not be sufficient to achieve all she wants. Her description of her life story suggests that her problem relating to men is long-lasting, possibly stemming from the loss of relationship

with her father and from the lack of a model of relationship between her mother and father in childhood.

Once Peta has been in therapy for a while and we both understand better the nature of the work to be done, we will regularly
review our work together, including the realism of her initial time-
scale. I foresee either that she will develop her awareness over six
months and leave, content with what she has achieved, or that she
will renegotiate her contract with me to work actively through the
experience of relationship with me for longer.

Peta is likely to use some of the established patterns of relationship with me in therapy that she has used towards others (including
men) in her past and present. For example, she may experience me
at times as an authority figure, or as withdrawing, in which case she
may 'withdraw', 'become silent', 'feel angry' or want to 'subvert my
authority' (her descriptions of such experiences). Some people with
these patterns withdraw from therapy precipitously – leaving themselves and their therapists with unresolved issues. To explore Peta's
awareness of this problem, I asked how she might subvert her therapy
or withdraw if she was unhappy with something I said or did. She
replied that she would have no intention of subverting her therapy
but might become 'silent' or 'guarded' and 'not walk out *yet*'. Her
answer confirmed my need to remain alert to times when she might
withdraw (rather than tell me directly what she was feeling), but it
reassured me she would not terminate abruptly. I would safeguard
against such an event by suggesting a leaving contract (see p. 32).

Other possible sources of difficulty could be my own unaware
patterns of relating. I anticipate staying alert to these by monitoring
my work in supervisory consultation, to learn as openly and clearly
as possible about the relationship processes that Peta and I co-create
together. The interacting (and transferential) patterns of relationship between client and therapist are further discussed below.

The course of therapy

Contracts

Clarifying working conditions is an important way of establishing a
'vessel' for the therapy. I will therefore probably 'make a contract'
with Peta during the initial sessions. I allow some flexibility regarding
the number of sessions needed to establish all the working conditions so that I can prioritize meeting the individual. I will reiterate
Peta's objectives, establishing an understanding regarding the areas
to be explored. I will explain Gestalt therapy and will discuss

arrangements regarding frequency, fees and arrangements for missed or cancelled sessions.

If Peta wants to continue after the initial session(s), I will probably offer her a contract for six weekly sessions with a review and the potential for re-contracting for a further period. If she then wants to remain in therapy with me, I will offer her either an open-ended contract or a contract for six months – the length of time she envisages staying in therapy from her present perspective. I will review Peta's therapy with her regularly, to update ourselves on what has been helpful or unhelpful, how her objectives have changed or been achieved. These reviews will be a natural part or pause in the therapy.

I will also negotiate an agreement about leaving therapy. For example, when she begins the first six-week contract, I will probably ask her to undertake to come back for at least one session to discuss the issues fully, should she decide to leave therapy suddenly. If she decides to enter into a longer-term contract, I will explain that leaving is an important part of the therapeutic process and suggest that she spends time on leaving, proportionate to the time spent in therapy.

I will discuss confidentiality with Peta and tell her the limits of confidentiality, and give her a written contract summarizing these conditions.

Form of therapy

Gestalt is by its very nature opposed to predicting the form that the therapy will take. In this phenomenological method, the therapist tries to *suspend* previous judgements and plans, in order to remain as open as possible to what is actually experienced, and to meet the individual, person to person, moment to moment, without preconceptions. I therefore *hypothesize* about some of the possible aims, directions and methods of therapy, rather than predict the unpredictable.

My aim is to heighten Peta's perception of her current functioning, including ways she helps to create her life circumstances or interrupts her own energy process, some of which may be wholly out of her awareness. This increase in awareness could help her develop a greater sense of options and better tools for relating to others, including men.

Therapy consists of a careful phenomenological exploration of her present experience within her life circumstances, including the immediate circumstances that are co-created by her and me. I will endeavour to ground this awareness in a dialogic relationship, in which we meet as two equals, each with different skills and expertise; and in which we can explore and study the very process of relating, of moving towards and separating in rhythmic alternation.

The primary methods of Gestalt therapy are:

- developing the conditions in which a dialogic relationship may evolve,
- using phenomenological methods of investigation of the field,
- using experiments to develop awareness of current functioning in the field.

Dialogic relationship

A dialogic relationship is one in which the uniqueness of each person is valued and where direct, mutual and open relations between persons are emphasized. It encompasses the 'I–Thou' and the 'I–It' styles of relating and the rhythmic alternation between them. The 'I–Thou' emphasizes natural connectedness and the 'I–It' natural separateness. Both are essential. Dialogue in this existential sense is not restricted to verbal contact but can take place in silence, laughter, movement and play as well as words.

A key premise in the Gestalt view of self is that we define and learn about our ever-changing selves in relationship to others; so the shifting relationship or dialogue between myself and Peta is a major way in which over time Peta can share different aspects of herself and thus further her awareness and development of self. Through this active exploration and study of our relationship, Peta may learn and internalize new relationship skills which she can use in other relationships.

Another essential concept is that the power to heal lies not in the therapist or even in the client alone, but in what happens *between* them, the contact between the two. Within the dialogic, the highest form of relating, with the greatest potential for healing, is the moment of mutual 'I–Thou' meeting. Yet paradoxically one cannot *aim* to establish 'I–Thou' contact. It can only arise out of preparation and grace. I will therefore prepare the ground for 'I–Thou' contact with Peta by practising the disciplines of inclusion, presence and commitment to non-exploitation, as described by Yontef (1980).

Inclusion signifies that I enter as fully as possible into Peta's subjective reality, without judging or analysing. At the same time, I retain a clear sense of myself. Practising presence means that I try to know myself as I am, rather than acting 'as if' I were someone else. I will sometimes choose to show myself by expressing my observations and responses, when I judge this clinically desirable (Jacobs 1989).

Commitment to non-exploitation indicates that I aim to treat Peta as an equal, and to develop a horizontal relationship, in which we speak the language of present-centred experiencing.

Using phenomenological methods of cooperative enquiry

The Gestalt field approach emphasizes that phenomenological reality is open to a multiplicity of interpretations. The meaning each individual gives to her perception of the world is unique. I cannot therefore know another's truth, so I try to avoid interpreting Peta's behaviour. Instead, I try to help her uncover her unique sense of meaning through description and investigation. I pay as much attention to the process, to the *way* she interacts, as to the content of the interaction. I attend to all aspects of her whole person and my own – shifting my attention between our facial, bodily, emotional responses and our verbal exchange and backgrounds. Holistic exploring of the ever-changing field cannot be represented in this chapter. However well done, the present description is inevitably reductionistic: it is static rather than evolving, and consists predominantly of words. It can only hint at the complex whole.

In practice, phenomenological enquiry means that I:

* bracket or set aside my previous assumptions so as to focus on immediate experience, whether Peta's or mine;
* describe immediate and concrete impressions, rather than explain or interpret;
* initially treat all aspects of the field described as equally significant, rather than assume any hierarchy of importance;
* invite Peta to explore, describe and research her own process of experience. (I find that asking 'How?' and 'What?' questions is more effective than 'Why?' questions in supporting the client to become interested in her own unfolding.)

Exploring the past

Attention to present process does not mean that I ignore Peta's past. There is often a mistaken impression that Gestalt therapists only deal with present phenomena. By paying close attention to Peta's present process and ways of interacting, pressing unfinished business from the past is likely to arise spontaneously. Using the Gestalt model, I can then offer Peta ways to bring those past situations alive in the present, to explore them actively and perhaps to find emotional resolution for them, thus finding and making herself anew, transforming her earlier decisions and image of herself, and freeing her to be more fully and flexibly involved in her present engagements with both men and women.

Using experiments to develop awareness

Gestalt therapy is exploratory and experimental from moment to moment, in the sense that neither therapist or client is controlling or able to predict the unfolding process of the session. In addition, Gestalt therapists and their clients sometimes design experiments *within* the overall experiment of the session, in which clients try out new behaviours and see what happens. Gestalt experiments may include creative and active elements, such as fantasy, visualization, exaggeration, role-playing, movement, drawing, dance, voice and language changes.

For example, I suggested a practical experiment to Peta in which she drew her brother and father playfighting and her 'inutterable fury of deprivation' (Fig. 2). She became deeply absorbed and voiced several new insights through the process of drawing. If Peta was in therapy with me, I might suggest that she extend that experiment in some way. I might ask her how she would like to extend it; for example, what the small figure of herself in the corner is doing or saying to herself.

I stress that experiments are not suggested in order to change Peta's behaviour but to further the cooperative investigation of her functioning and increase her awareness of aspects of herself. The challenge for me is to co-design experiments with Peta, which are real enough to provoke her unaware feelings and yet 'safe' enough for her to be willing to try them.

Possible priorities

Currently, Peta presents herself predominantly through her cognitive abilities and interests. In her search for more satisfying and intimate relationships, it may ultimately be important to her to become equally familiar with her emotional and physical range. However, she must have learned to deflect from her emotional self for some very good reasons. So I would not start by trying to get Peta 'in touch with her feelings' (often the stereotype associated with Gestalt therapy); instead, I would address myself to those aspects where she is currently vital and urgent – for example, her wish to discuss the importance of gender. I am interested to find out what Peta's views are and how she sees gender issues affecting her own life and the lives of others, as well as her relationships to men. I might share some of my experiences, views and reading (Polster 1993), so as to engage with her on a theme that is very important to her and which she feels others have often ignored.

I imagine that I will also do considerable work initially with visualization and creative media, as Peta responded very readily to such suggestions. Depending upon the experience of these initial explorations, I might *gradually* help Peta to explore the sensations and emotions associated with the discussion, visualization and creative work.

I do not work with experiments in isolation but always in the context of the dialogic relationship and in the field that therapist and client co-create. This emphasis upon relationship is especially important to Peta, who has described difficulties with relationship and a tendency to withdraw automatically as a way of dealing with stress. Hopefully with me she will have a new experience of relationship in which she can risk trying new options, and internalize the experience so that she can experiment outside the therapy session.

Transferential processes within a field approach

It is commonly supposed that Gestalt therapists have no theory of transference (Kovel 1976) and do not work with transferential processes. This is again a misunderstanding. Historically, Gestalt therapists have not objected to the *concept* of transference or the need to understand the complex interaction of transference and countertransference. They have, on the other hand, criticized what they saw as the over-emphasis upon the transferential relationship, upon interpretation as the prime method of working with it, and the consequent devaluation of the person-to-person relationship and other aspects of the whole field.

Not surprisingly, people usually reproduce in the therapeutic relationship patterns of relating that they manifest in other parts of their life. If that seems to happen between Peta and me, I would not simply identify it as transference but instigate a cooperative enquiry in which we could together explore the different possible meanings and values of that behaviour. For example, when I first read the transcript, I felt irritated by Peta's circumlocutory style. I wondered about the processes involved in my reaction, including transferential and counter-transferential phenomena (Clarkson 1992). Where does this irritation belong? Does this style of talking perhaps remind me of some figure from my past towards whom I have unresolved feelings? Is my irritation a response to the way that Peta is actively configuring the field? If the latter, I wonder what meaning this could have for Peta's whole self in context? Is Peta perhaps unawarely irritated, and disowning that irritation? Is she unconsciously inviting others to feel the irritation towards her? Or is she communicating something important to me about her previous experiences of relationship? Have significant others felt irritation towards her? At this stage I have no conclusions – only questions which I anticipate gradually exploring with Peta.

A cooperative investigation would not consist of primarily cognitive ruminations over the origins of the feeling of irritation, but could involve holistic phenomenological and experimental investigation as explained above and illustrated by the following example. Intrigued by Peta's long unfinished sentences, I might for instance suggest that she experiment by completing every sentence. I think it is quite likely that Peta would find this hard. But in doing so and especially in exploring the difficulties she encounters we might find out more about the meaning that her incomplete sentences have for her. If Peta is hesitant, I will perhaps scale the experiment down and adapt it to integrate her comments; or stay with her disinclination and explore that. Peta's response to one investigative comment I made about her style of speech suggests that this could indeed be a fruitful and charged area to explore. Moira had said: 'She is immediately responsive. She smiles and laughs. It makes sense to her; there is a good and real connection and contact. This statement touches her and she says, "It's quite scary . . . a lot of mileage in that".'

The beauty of a phenomenological approach based on field theory is that we initially treat all aspects of the field as equally significant. We move between layers and levels of the field or life space, switching frames or positions and employing a wonderfully creative and varied range of methods of exploration, as needed:

> We can reach deeply into the past in a regressive re-enactment on one occasion, while at another time, in different conditions, we . . . look purely at the present relationship with the therapist, today in this room now. We can switch from reality to role play, from experiencing something at a physical bodily level, to visual fantasy, to searching for metaphor, to telling the story (Polster 1987). Gestalt therapists need to take account of the state of the entire field conditions at the time. What is a skilful therapeutic challenge at one point, will be ineffective or un-creative at another . . . We can move playfully between levels, ages, parts of the body, regions of the field, or alternatively stay

still – focusing in a meditative way, simply following the moving focus of the unfolding present.

(Parlett 1993)

Problem areas

It is as contrary to the phenomenological approach to predict problem areas as it is to map the course of therapy. Again I share my hypotheses rather than predict.

A possible problem area could be that one of Peta's main reasons for considering therapy and for wanting to explore and resolve her problems with men is that she wants to be a better counsellor. Although this is a very worthy motivation, I have found that people usually need personal energy and commitment in order to really engage in the hard work of knowing themselves better. It does seem that Peta also has personal determination to explore and sort out her problems; so I imagine her wish to be a better counsellor is only a part of her motivation and sounds like a fine initial reason for coming into therapy.

'Resistance'

If Peta chooses to come into Gestalt therapy, she is likely to start by embracing the attention to her present functioning and the participation in active experimentation which are the hallmarks of that approach. But at some point she will inevitably express some form of ambivalence or inner conflict regarding the therapeutic exploration.

I do not see a client's reluctance to try things as a problem area so much as the very essence of therapy. Gestalt places a high value on the client's so-called 'resistance'. What now appears to be 'resistance' was almost certainly once a life-enhancing decision, a creative adjustment to difficult circumstances in the past. I do not therefore try to dissolve or overcome any hesitant or 'resisting' forces; instead, I will heighten and concentrate upon those forces with Peta, exploring their somatic, intellectual and emotional aspects, to find out their meaning to her or their significance in our interaction. This concentration ensures that the individual actually experiences her so-called 'resistances' as belonging to her and as much part of her as whatever it is they resist (Perls *et al.* 1973).

For example, Peta described a tendency to 'subvert' authority figures rather than to express direct disagreement. As indicated earlier, I suppose that Peta may 'subvert' the process of therapy in some way. I need to be alert to this (through supervision as well as

self-monitoring) and ready to bring 'subversive' behaviour to awareness, so that together we may explore its meaning or value to her.
I am also interested in what she means by subversive. Some so-
called subversive skills have very creative sides to them. Although
this may be a problem, it is also an area with great potential: Peta
may have invested some of her vital life energy in 'subversive' skills.
Exploring her tendency to 'subvert' may enable her to understand
it, and free her to use that energy in other ways.

Because the exploration of 'problem areas' is so central to the
Gestalt approach, I have also explored various other 'problem' issues
under the headings 'Assessment' and 'The course of therapy'.

Criteria for successful outcome

My criteria for success are based in two broad areas: our cooperative
evaluation of Peta's objectives, and analysis of the vitality of her
process of contact or figure/ground formation.

Evaluation of Peta's objectives

I will monitor and evaluate the success of Peta's therapy in an ongoing
way, not just at the end of therapy. It is important to build in
regular reviews of the therapeutic process, in which we both discuss
the progress she is making (or not), and decide whether she wishes
to continue with me, carry on her journey with another therapist or
stop and agree any necessary adjustments in the approach and
methods.

At these regular reviews, as well as towards the end of therapy, we
would evaluate cooperatively her progress in terms of her objectives
and desired outcomes. My criteria for therapeutic progress emphasize the importance of the client (affirmed by the therapist) recognizing her own standards and values.

Assessment of the vitality of Peta's contact process

Perls *et al.* (1973) suggest that a definition of 'normal behaviour' is
unnecessary because of the observable qualities of the individual's
contact process. When the figure of the individual's present contact
or interaction is lacking in energy, we may be sure that something
vital is being blocked out of her awareness. Peta herself can therefore judge her own progress by noticing whether or not she experiences heightened vitality, more effective functioning or a deeper
sense of meaning.

An additional criterion is whether the client's therapist and her friends notice the changes that she feels subjectively. In Gestalt theory, a vital function of the self is the formation of figures of contact or meaning against the background of the rest of a person's life circumstances. This self process is the organizing principle by which the individual creates order and meaning from the diversity of processes that constitute the ever-changing universe. If the individual's process of figure–background formation is weak, the figure of contact is dull or confused. Other people are not drawn to it or to the person manifesting it. When, on the other hand, an individual re-establishes a dynamic process of figure–background formation, the figure is interesting, bright and energetic, so that people are naturally responsive: 'The process of figure/background formation is a dynamic one in which the urgencies and resources of the field progressively lend their powers to the interest, brightness and force of the dominant figure' (Perls *et al.* 1973: 278).

If Peta's process of contact becomes more dynamic, people will experience her increased contact, vitality and commitment to life in their own responses to her. I will also monitor my own responses to her. In my experience, it is a common occurrence for a client who is beginning to make progress to report that a friend (who does not even know that she is in therapy) has spontaneously told her how much and in what ways she has changed.

Once Peta has explored her styles of relating with me and developed her relationship skills, she might perhaps refer herself (with my support) to work with a male therapist for a further period.

Summary

The rich, complex and integrative nature of the Gestalt approach does not mean that it is indiscriminately eclectic. Gestalt practice is flexible, creative and spontaneous, and yet it rests upon a clear theoretical model.

I believe that there are less differences between the different schools of psychotherapy than some of the adherents of the different schools would admit. Many of us are essentially doing and being in similar ways, but using different theoretical constructs and language to describe our experiences. I am not, however, arguing for eclecticism or even necessarily for integrative training, at least initially. Learning a psychotherapeutic approach is like learning to play an instrument or speak a foreign language. It is important to learn to play each instrument well, but it is also quite possible to play another instrument or to understand something of how one instrument relates to others.

I am tired of hearing other psychotherapists reduce and trivialize Gestalt (Kovel 1976), while at the same time enthusing about 'new' theoretical contributions that have been essential aspects of the Gestalt approach since the 1940s and 1950s. Some of the early innovative Gestalt concepts have either been unconsciously assimilated into the mainstream of psychodynamic psychotherapy or have been re-invented during the last two decades when psychoanalysis has found new life, particularly through developments in Object Relations and self psychology (Clarkson and Mackewn 1993: ch. 5). I am equally tired of hearing humanistic psychotherapists assume that all psychoanalytic approaches emphasize the 'blank screen' of the therapist, despite the enormous differences between analytic disciplines, and despite research which indicates that the client experiences different approaches as approximately equally successful (Smith *et al.* 1980).

Gestalt is a fine instrument which I have learned one can play well. I find it a useful means of conceptualizing my work with Peta and others. But Gestalt psychotherapy – like all the other therapies represented in this book – is only one model or map of human nature and relationship. Let us not mistake the map for the territory and get so lost in partisan debate about the advantages of the different schools of psychotherapy that we lose sight of the questing, changing human beings we all are.

In this instance, it is essential we do not lose sight of you, Peta. I hope this experiment in which you have played the central part has proved valuable to you. I would have preferred to *meet* you, rather than to write *about* you. I look forward to hearing your responses.

Further reading

American Psychiatric Association (1987). *Diagnostic and Statistical Manual of Mental Disorder: DSM-III-R*. Washington, DC: APA.

Beisser, A.R. (1970). The paradoxical theory of change. In J. Fagan and I. Shepherd (Eds), *Gestalt Therapy Now*. Palo Alto, CA: Science and Behavior Books.

Clarkson, P. (1992). *Transactional Analysis Psychotherapy: An Integrated Approach*. London: Tavistock/Routledge.

Clarkson, P. and Mackewn, J. (1993). *Fritz Perls*. London: Sage.

Hycner, R.H. (1985). Dialogical Gestalt therapy: An initial proposal. *Gestalt Journal*, Vol. 13, No. 1, pp. 23–49.

Jacobs, L. (1989). Dialogue in Gestalt theory and therapy. *Gestalt Journal*, Vol. 12, No. 1, pp. 25–68.

Kovel, J. (1976). *A Complete Guide to Therapy*. London: Penguin.

Parlett, M. (1993). Towards a more Lewinian Gestalt therapy. *British Gestalt Journal*, Vol. 2, No. 2, pp. 115–21.

Perls, F.S., Hefferline, R.F. and Goodman, P. (1973). *Gestalt Therapy: Excitement and Growth in the Human Personality*. London: Penguin.

Polster, E. (1987). *Every Person's Life is Worth a Novel*. New York: W.W. Norton.

Polster, M. (1993). *Eve's Daughters: The Forbidden Heroism of Women*. San Francisco, CA: Jossey-Bass.

Smith, M.L., Glass, G.V. and Miller, T.I. (1980). *The Benefits of Psychotherapy*. Baltimore, MD: Johns Hopkins University Press.

Yontef, G.M. (1980). Gestalt therapy: A dialogic method. Unpublished manuscript.

Yontef, G.M. (1988). Assimilating diagnostic and psychoanalytic perspectives into Gestalt therapy. *Gestalt Journal*, Vol. 11, No. 1, pp. 5–32.

Zinker, J. (1978). *Creative Process in Gestalt Therapy*. New York: Vintage Books.

JUDY MOORE

PERSON-CENTRED PSYCHOTHERAPY

The therapist

I was trained in the person-centred tradition over a two-and-a-half year period by FDI (Britain), now PCT (Britain). Since the completion of my training in 1988, I have worked as an individual therapist purely within that tradition and primarily within the context of a Student Counselling Service. I now also tutor a postgraduate diploma course in person-centred counselling. In our training we use the terms 'counselling' and 'therapy' interchangeably as I do throughout this chapter.

When I work with individuals I do not try to integrate methods or insights from any other tradition, although I would not place myself at the 'purest' end of person-centred therapy as defined by Barbara Temaner Brodley. This means I do not hold back from practices such as asking questions nor from making connections that I perceive between different aspects of a client's experiencing if I believe it might be useful to the therapeutic process. I also consider introducing 'focusing' into sessions with clients where I believe it can be helpful. The practice of focusing, developed originally by Eugene Gendlin in the late 1960s and early 1970s and adopted by some person-centred practitioners, involves inviting the client to focus on her inner 'felt sense' and guiding her through a series of steps that may bring about a significant affective shift in relation to a particular issue. I find this very helpful where a client is stuck, particularly in intellectualizing specific concerns.

Although I see my primary mode of working as being within the affective domain, I have great respect for the intellect as part of the whole person. Prior to entering the counselling world, I spent many years studying and teaching English literature and most of my current therapeutic work is with students. I have also been closely involved, first as a counsellor and subsequently as a tutor, with the Open University Women's Studies course. I am myself a feminist and accept many of Peta's insights into her own situation. I also believe that what Peta perceives as 'her' problem with men is inevitable in a society where most men are unable to handle close emotional relationships. I am certainly willing to engage with Peta on these issues, if and when it feels right, because a feminist understanding is part of our shared perceptual world.

A central tenet of the person-centred approach is to equalize power between therapist and client. Temaner Brodley's concern is that if a person-centred practitioner deviates from empathy and acceptance, then she may become abusive in the use of her own person (i.e. her congruence) in the therapeutic interaction. My own fear is that if the therapist is not fully in touch with her own experiencing or is unwilling to be real in the therapeutic encounter, then she is equally in danger of becoming abusive through what I regard as a parody of empathy and acceptance. Self-monitoring and a willingness to be myself in the relationship are therefore very important to me. I regard them as necessary if the other two core conditions are to be trustworthy. My main concern is to establish a climate of trust and acceptance so that it is possible for the client to extend her perceptual field to encompass feelings and insights that are currently being denied awareness. It is for the client to find her own route to greater integration according to the person-centred belief that 'authority about the client lies in the client and not in an outside expert' (Mearns and Thorne 1988: 18). I see myself principally as a companion on a journey of self-discovery.

Further information requested

It was very difficult for me to formulate questions to ask Peta, not because there were not areas where I felt it would be helpful to know more, but because it is so counter to my usual way of working to bombard a client with questions at the outset of a relationship. In order to participate in this project, however, I came up with a number of questions which might represent areas that I would normally expect to explore through empathic responding. Some of my questions were evidently red herrings. For example, I am not certain how helpful it is to me to know that Peta's counselling orientation is the same as my own! However, I learnt a great deal from most of her responses and began to build up a picture of where our work together might lead.

I was interested to know in greater detail about Peta's relationships with men and what seems to go wrong with them. I asked
about the problem with men she had been having 'over the last few
weeks' as she put it the original interview. Her response reveals
more about her feelings of being ignored by Ed on the counselling
certificate course:

> I wanted from him a simple acknowledgement that I had
> been heard, that I was struggling with feelings that I wanted
> to understand; that I wasn't picking on him, but he
> represented something I needed to bounce off, but what I
> got back was something quite different, so I felt all the time
> that my needs were not actually being heard.

In response to a separate question about what was the 'more' she
wanted from Ed or Hamish, Peta is even more explicit, making her
own connection between current need and past deprivation:

> To be paid attention. Sometimes I think that, in the way of
> things, I wanted in childhood the kind of attention I never
> got perhaps, which has the weight of, the feel of colossal
> psychic need which I'm sure they must have picked up, that
> sometimes I was not in touch with, but some things I knew
> was going on. Latterly I wanted something much simpler,
> possibly something profounder, which was an indication that
> I had . . . that my need had been registered.

I asked about some of the 'phases and crises' that her marriage
had been through. Peta revealed that she married because she 'didn't
actually know what else to do'. Quite soon within the marriage she
was 'desperately, desperately unhappy', geographically isolated and
regularly left alone by her husband at weekends. He would go off
shooting, ignoring her unhappiness, but probably equally confused:
'I didn't really understand it; he didn't really understand it'.

The pain of abandonment that she had experienced during her
marriage was evidently recalled for her on holiday in France with
the lover who 'used silence as a weapon'. I asked what she thought
was 'damaging' for her about this man. It sounds as if she was
deeply hurt by him and his inability to communicate, which she
attributes to there being 'a lot of things in his past . . . he hadn't
talked about' (e.g. he had lost a child, been married and divorced).
This led to 'a great sense in which all discussions about sadness or
difficulty or being in relationship or any emotional states, any feelings
at all, all of those were difficult'. Peta's way of dealing with a very
traumatic row they had in France was to withdraw into herself 'by
an act of will': '[I] completed myself for self-protection, became

inaccessible and went on'. This withdrawal concealed 'great suffer-ing' and a strong desire to hurt him: 'I *wanted* to hurt him, I wanted to [*very forcefully said*] *make him hurt as I had been hurt'*.

I also asked Peta if she could say a little more about the *patterns* she got into in relationships with men (she had said that the rela-tionship with her lover had got 'a sort of shape to it'). She replied:

> ... it's clamouring for attention, it's saying 'Listen to me', and it must be very difficult for blokes to listen to me [*last few words very quiet*] when they are not, well, when it feels like I'm attacking, a threat – and I'm often a threat ... [But] if a person's needs go on not being recognized, not being heard, there's a constant feeling of being thwarted ... You know, this person who is meant to be my male parent is actually not talking to anyone, actually physically not there ...

In response to a later question ('What does a man's silence mean to you?'), Peta links her own silent withdrawal to the withdrawal she has experienced in various men in her life. In France, before her withdrawal, she had felt 'consumed with rage', and can infer from this that a man's silence is likely to conceal anger: 'I can plot it and say he must be really pissed off about something 'cause I'm getting this brick wall, so what's behind the brick wall?' She also links withdrawal to a film she had seen illustrating Bowlby's theories about maternal deprivation, where withdrawal is related to despair. She says that in France she 'was absolutely consumed with the same quality' and observes that it is only 'now' that she connects the two events.

In response to a separate question, Peta talks at some length and very lovingly about her relationship with her son. She is accepting of his becoming more independent of her, but talks about being 'ripped apart' when he first stayed away for the night without tell-ing her. When asked about 'coalitions and equality' in her own adolescence, she talks about having been 'extremely depressed ... at various points' and 'suicidal at one point'. The 'coalition' she most feels is lacking in her current life is a sexual partnership with a man. Later she talks about an aspect of her sexuality which has not been cultivated as being 'a sharing, a mutuality which happens in a decent relationship'.

On reading the initial interview, I felt that being bullied at school was probably a key area to explore, and I asked if Peta could say a little more about being bullied and about how she had experienced boredom 'physically' as a child. She admits to not having dealt with the feelings, and although there were obvious social reasons for her being different, she 'almost expected to be bullied' through 'a learnt defeatism'. She continues:

> I *can't* look at that, and *won't*... I'm not prepared to deal with that, but I think that I would deal with that in therapy. It's really a pile of horse shit actually.

At this point in the interview, there is some discussion about whether she would like a break, and she comments that 'that last thing was a bit difficult and I hadn't realized quite until now'. In response to my next question, Peta talks about her adolescence as 'a plateau of dissociation'. People regarded her as 'just terribly stupid' while she lived for 'years and years and years... in a complete dream world'. She goes on to describe boredom as 'a kind of sickness':

> I don't know whether you can describe the feeling of rejection in physical terms... It's a kind of yearning, a longing thing, but there's a kind of inevitable... You'll *never* get through it, you'll never... The block is much too big and wide.

The remaining questions that seem of relevance were about Peta's feminism. She talks about how her conditioning as a woman had left her without sufficient confidence in herself or 'drive' to make a career in textile design. The career she then followed in teaching was hampered by her responsibilities as a single parent and by her being offered the fodder of many women's professional lives: 'temporary contracts; somebody else's maternity leaves; supply teaching'. The cumulative effect of this she acknowledges as 'demeaning'. Lack of professional respect 'compounds the problem... and makes it more difficult to be taken seriously and to take myself seriously'. She talks about this question as opening 'a can of worms', and remarks: 'I'm sure a lot of the flack I threw out was because I felt dismissed; which I guess was true'. More recently, she has evolved a spiritual awareness through Quakerism that permits her to recognize 'that the divine is in every person' and is for her most accessible through black women writers and feminist poets. The love and support of other women has clearly sustained her through the isolation she has experienced in her more difficult relationships with men.

Assessment

It feels very strange to me to have so much information about Peta without having met her and without having established a relationship with her. I am aware of the importance of her trusting Moira

Walker in her being willing to answer my questions so fully. Normally, I would not expect to know so much about a client until after (perhaps) several months, over which time I hope she would be able to explore deeper and more difficult areas within the context of a safe therapeutic relationship.

The first assumption I must make about Peta is one that I would make about any client who presents themselves for therapy: that there is some level of incongruence between her inner experiencing and her self-concept. It is the discomfort arising from this incongruence that creates readiness for therapy. Peta states one level of this incongruence very clearly in the first two paragaphs of the original interview. Her opening sentence is 'I've got a problem with men' and she goes on to acknowledge that she feels 'self-conscious and rather uncomfortable' about saying she is a feminist. The anguish of her position becomes more evident as the interview progresses, culminating in the paradox of her desire to say, 'Give me equality. I demand it!' and her recognition that 'it pains me that men I respect turn away from me so soon. Because they feel disempowered'.

A further and more visible aspect of her incongruence emerges towards the end of the interview where Peta talks about how she no longer wants to be seen as 'confident':

I'm seen as confident because that's how I come across. Kurt
Vonnegut said we have to be careful how we seem to be;
and I am. And I'm learning more and more how to be
careful because I don't actually want to be seen as confident.
It doesn't actually match . . . congruence.

In her willingness to be more fully known by others and to access a wider range of feelings and needs than her self-concept as a feminist might have permitted, Peta is clearly on the edge of much deeper self-discovery. She recognizes the limits of her own socio-political analysis and hence of her capacity for reducing the pain of experiencing by intellectual understanding:

I'm getting *tired* of being turned away from, so I'm actually
getting angry, and I realize that when I'm faced with silence,
or with a low key emotional response . . . I find it not only
threatening but traumatizing . . .

In terms of person-centred theory, what is happening is that the healthiest part of herself, what Rogers terms 'the actualizing tendency', is asserting itself through Peta's feelings, in this instance feelings of weariness, anger, threat and trauma. The power of these emergent feelings undoubtedly lies in a complex web of past experiences, woven only in part from the socially constructed aspects of reality that are readily accessible to feminist analysis. The discomfort of her present position, which seems likely to have been exacerbated by the increased self-awareness she has developed through the counselling skills course, makes it possible for her to consider confronting extremely painful aspects of her past.

Rogers believed that the actualizing tendency is the drive towards health and the full accomplishment of the *whole* human organism, but that this basic motivation is generally impeded by *parts* of the organism, particularly those concerned with self-perception. It is clear, even from the relatively small amount of information we have about Peta's early life, that she began to conceptualize herself as different from her peers and therefore unacceptable to them ('I was brought up with a middle-class accent . . . But I was put into a school that was not like that'). When she later talks about being bullied, she speaks of a 'learned defeatism'. It seems as if aspects of this have stayed with her into adulthood, being recalled, for example, when she speaks of lacking confidence to pursue an artistic career, or finding it hard 'to take myself seriously'.

In the course of therapy, I anticipate that the actualizing tendency will enable more and more of Peta's true feelings and needs to become accessible to her. Rogers believed that:

> . . . human beings in some measure possess the capacity and have the natural tendency to reorganize and reconstruct their self-concepts in order to make them more congruent with the totality of their experience.
>
> (Thorne 1992: 35)

From what she has told us so far, the aspects of the self-concept which seem most likely to change are those which relate to her perception of her feminism, her 'incongruent' presentation of herself to others as more confident than she really feels, and her sometimes negative view of her own abilities.

Another key area which I believe will play a significant part in the course of Peta's therapy is the presenting issue of her desire for close, equal and fulfilling relationships with men. This I anticipate as being a very difficult area to disentangle, because it seems likely that part of the problem must relate to Peta's own tendency to feel frustrated when she is unheard. She then relates angrily and eventually withdraws. It may also be that the men with whom she tries to relate are themselves incapable of intimate relationship.

It is clear that the therapeutic relationship itself will be a kind of testing ground for this very complicated area. There is a sufficient amount of common ground between Peta and myself to indicate that it should be relatively easy to establish a good relationship or therapeutic alliance. I have already indicated that I have some understanding of Peta's feminist perspective on her experiencing, particularly in close relationships with men. I also have one child, who is a boy, and think I could understand very well something of the intensity of her relationship with Andy. I found myself very moved by her description of her spirituality and how it may find expression through individual women writers, something which again I can identify with from my own experience. At the same time, I am currently fascinated by the whole notion of the spiritual dimension of human experiencing, partly because this is an area we address in the counselling training with which I am involved. My feelings towards Peta – particularly from her responses to my questions – are, on the whole, very warm and positive; although, because I spend a considerable part of my time in a teaching role, I feel somewhat threatened by her acknowledged desire to 'subvert facilitators'. Stepping back from this, I can see that it relates to issues around power and Peta's desire to claim personal power for herself, but I am left with some feelings of unease, possibly related to Peta's use of the term 'subvert'. To me this implies a covert undermining, rather than a direct attack that could be more cleanly dealt with. Yet in this discomfort itself there are opportunities for growth, as I believe that we could establish a sufficiently good relationship to deal constructively with these and other negative feelings that would inevitably arise in both of us.

Therapeutic possibilities

Although I do not regard it as necessary to have things in common with my clients, I find it helps, particularly in the early stages of the relationship, if some kind of rapport can be established, if I can demonstrate fairly quickly some empathic understanding of the client's perceptual world. My aim in attempting to achieve such a rapport is to establish a working therapeutic alliance. Once this has taken place, I am more likely to be perceived as a 'resourceful' ally to the client, and our work together can really begin (Barrett-Lennard 1988: 12). There are, however, dangers in empathic identification, and I am particularly wary of how strongly moved I was by Peta's description of being 'ripped apart' by her son's growing independence, as I immediately feel sad at the thought of my own son growing away from me. This is something I would clearly need to look at in supervision, as I would also need to consider my own experiencing of emotionally uncommunicative men and my sense of vulnerability in the role of facilitator. My potential for general responsiveness to Peta and therefore my capacity for forming a successful therapeutic alliance with her is probably high, but perhaps dangerous in some areas.

I think that Peta is very 'ripe' for therapy. She is sufficiently in touch with her own feelings to make a moment-by-moment awareness of what is going on for her much more possible than I experience with many clients at the beginning of the counselling relationship. She talks freely about loving, being angry (e.g. 'the *unspeakable* fury of deprivation' with her father), hurting and wanting to hurt (the lover in France), wanting attention and a 'yearning, a longing' for connection. There were several opportunities for empathic responding during the initial interview, where Peta's narrative might have been interrupted to explore feelings that were coming to the surface (e.g. 'When I needed coalitions and equality there was nothing . . . I think I am *very angry* about that now'). It seems to me that there is much that is surfacing in Peta, and much that is on the edge of awareness which can be accessed by careful empathy.

Although it is difficult to be certain as to what level of unconditional positive regard I could offer Peta, I have already felt sufficiently moved by her to make me optimistic about being able to develop and sustain warmth towards her and acceptance of all aspects of her experiencing. Her feminism would certainly not intimidate me: as I have indicated, it would make it rather easier for me to engage with her. I can, however, foresee some problem areas, which might seriously challenge the relationship or cause Peta to withdraw. To these I will return in the following sections.

Peta's past history of being bullied, her difficulty with authority figures, her commitment to feminism, her expressed frustration with 'the blank screen in therapy', and her awareness of her own incongruence are all factors which make it clear to me that I need to be very open and trustworthy in the relationship, very clearly myself. The sharing of power, to which the person-centred approach is committed, seems of crucial significance here and, if I should fail in achieving this, I think the relationship would fail.

Two factors in Peta's recent and current life suggest to me that her therapy is likely to reach a 'successful' outcome (although the question of what constitutes 'success' is not a simple one). The first is that some kind of process seems to have already begun through her counselling certificate course, raising very clearly her 'problem with men'. The second is that she has support outside the therapeutic relationship in terms of good women friends and her own spiritual awareness. These factors suggest that she is already committed to her own process, and would be receiving sufficient nurture outside of the counselling room to enable her to stay with the very painful issues that are likely to emerge in the unfolding of that process.

The course of therapy

As I have already indicated, I would normally expect the knowledge that I now have of Peta to emerge gradually over a quite considerable period of time. I should also make it clear that I rarely conceptualize how I am working with a client, or analyse what is going on with her in terms of person-centred theory as I have done in the last section. My main concern is to offer the core conditions to the best of my ability, and this means being fully present for the client. An excessive concern with theory or process I have found only to impede the quality of my presence.

I would hope to have met Peta without prior knowledge so that I could simply be with her, trusting the unfolding of different levels of feeling to determine what happens in individual sessions and in the course of the therapy as a whole. At each stage, my concern is with what is coming up for the client in the present moment. The significance of working with the present is explained by Carl Rogers in the following terms:

> We have come to recognize that if we can provide understanding of the way the client seems to himself at this moment, he can do the rest. The therapist must lay aside his preoccupation with diagnosis and his diagnostic shrewdness, must discard his tendency to make professional evaluations, must cease his endeavours to formulate an accurate prognosis, must give up the temptation subtly to guide the individual, and must concentrate on one purpose only; that of providing deep understanding and acceptance of the attitudes consciously held at this moment by the client as he explores step by step into the dangerous areas which he has been denying to consciousness.
>
> (Rogers 1951: 30)

I cannot see any reason why I would deviate from my usual way of working with Peta, although I can identify a few areas where particular care might be required. I explore some of these below.

I would introduce myself very briefly at the beginning of the first session, explain that we have approximately fifty minutes together, to be used as she wishes. At the end of the session, I would invite her to return if she wishes. If asked, I would describe how I work and explain the principles behind the person-centred approach. Although I have some sense from the information I have been given that the therapy is likely to take some months, or possibly a year or more, I might not have been so clear at the end of a first session with Peta. I would instead suggest that she return for as long as it seems helpful to her, indicating either at this point or at as early a stage as possible, that I am open both as to the frequency and the duration of our sessions.

I would try to give expression to my own positive and any persistent negative feelings towards Peta, believing that if these are left unexpressed they will undermine our relationship. I would try to be accepting of all Peta's feelings and all aspects of her experiencing, although her defences might make her as difficult for me as she seems at times to have been for her counselling certificate facilitators. I would try to be consistently accepting of her as a person in order to break the cycle of defensive behaviour that drives people (men in particular) away from her. It may well be that I would not succeed in this, particularly as the relationship between us becomes more important and deeper issues emerge. Peta may well then choose to test the relationship beyond limits that it could take.

I sense, however, that empathy may be the core condition that is initially most difficult to get 'right' for Peta. She clearly at times behaves in ways that make it difficult to hear what is really going on for her. For example, she talks in response to one of my questions about throwing out 'all this flack' to Ed, one of the facilitators on the counselling certificate course. Yet what she wanted from him was 'a simple acknowledgement that I had been heard, that I was struggling with feelings that I wanted to understand'. Later she talks about wanting from her facilitators 'an indication . . . that my need had been registered'. I can imagine that I might well find it difficult to 'register' Peta's 'need' if I were myself under attack by her. Perhaps in such an instance it might be important to register a congruent response before I would be capable of giving an empathic one. Without giving expression to my own response to being attacked, I could certainly not maintain genuine acceptance.

It also seems to me that there is some ambivalence in Peta as to *how far* she really wants to be heard. She obviously desperately wants to be understood; and yet, probably because of past abuse and isolation, too deep a level of understanding may be perceived by her as an assault. This seems to have happened with the art therapy tutor who made 'various psychodynamic interventions in personal territory that I found deeply, deeply threatening, and I withdrew'. Because of Peta's 'ripeness' for therapy and the fact that she demonstrates a willingness to accept uncomfortable feelings, there might be a danger of plunging in too deep too soon, causing her to withdraw, possibly from the therapy altogether. It is clear that she is organized and likes to be in charge of the material she presents, so it would remain vital throughout that she present what she is ready to present and retains a sense of being in charge of her own emergent process. It might be important initially to keep the empathy fairly light, reflecting back surface meaning or the quality and intensity of *expressed* feeling rather than seeking too much for feelings at or beneath the edge of conscious awareness. Later, with more trust in the relationship, it should be possible to go deeper.

I cannot foresee that focusing is an option I would take in working with Peta, although it might emerge as a possible way forward in relation to a specific issue. Although I find it an extremely powerful method of accessing feelings on the edge of awareness, I would suggest it to Peta only if she trusted me implicitly.

The end of therapy would be determined by Peta, and this may or may not come at a point I am happy with. Ideally, it would come at a time when she felt she had worked through enough to be living in a more comfortable and congruent way, more in touch with the totality of her experiencing, and able to integrate into her self-concept those aspects of herself which she currently finds unacceptable. It may be, however, that Peta would choose to terminate the relationship after having resolved only some issues, but then decide to re-enter therapy after a break of weeks, months or possibly years. In such a case, I would always be willing to pick up working with her if it were practically possible, just as I would be ready, in the case of a more 'complete' termination, to see her in times of future crisis.

Problem areas

One of my concerns is that, because of having been abused in a considerable number of relationships in the past, Peta may be particularly vulnerable at the point where the counselling relationship begins to deepen. A therapeutic alliance can develop or a relationship can simply falter at quite an early stage:

> The alliance evolves unevenly but overall toward deeper engagement, increasing eventfulness and greater commitment . . . Alternatively, such development never really takes off, or it begins to and then falters and ceases or is aborted by circumstances.
> (Barrett-Lennard 1988: 13)

It is at this point that I anticipate she may well become particularly challenging or testing, possibly even 'subversive' to the point of undermining the relationship before it is strong enough to weather such testing. She has made several references already to her capacity for 'withdrawal' and even 'dissociation' (during the years of being bullied). While getting beyond her 'withdrawal' threshold would clearly be a real turning point, I must accept that there is quite a strong possibility that she may instead choose not to take this step. Such an early withdrawal would auger less well for her returning to therapy after a break than her withdrawal from a strong, close, good relationship.

Another area of potential difficulty in terms of the therapeutic process is Peta's ability to conceptualize her experience in terms of feminist theory. I have found that it is extremely helpful to understand that many aspects of my own life have actually been conditioned by the fact that I am a woman. Such understanding has enabled me to feel less pain and confusion over the fact that, like Peta, I have spent a considerable part of my life putting my own career second to family needs. Similarly, understanding that most men are conditioned not to relate on a close emotional level has helped me to blame myself less when relationships with men have faltered through lack of communication. There is, however, a negative side to such understanding, in that it can detract from the full impact and complexity of the feelings involved. Since working with feelings is the essence of my approach, it would be necessary to get beyond understanding of the issues within *any* conceptual framework. For example, in describing her painful experience with the lover in France, Peta is evidently aware of possible reasons for his withdrawal ('a lot of things in his past . . . he hadn't talked about'). She can relate the pattern to her not being heard by other significant men in her life, thus tacitly raising the considerable gender issue of women's invisibility to men. This is a fascinating and engaging issue, but, in terms of person-centred practice, it is much more important to validate Peta's feelings in relation to specific occasions when she has been ignored by men ('I wanted to make him hurt as I had been hurt', 'there's a constant feeling of being thwarted'). It is such validation that releases more feelings and enables the therapeutic process to unfold. It is a very delicate operation to affirm a client's intellectual understanding while encouraging the unfolding of her feeling responses to specific issues. It is too easy, within my tradition, to dismiss intellectual understanding (which would, incidentally, demonstrate considerable lack of acceptance), and I have a slight concern that, because of Peta's access to 'socio-political analysis' and my own interest in feminist theory, I may over-engage on this level with some neglect of empathy.

I believe that the person-centred approach is one that could work with Peta because it involves working respectfully with the client at her own pace. I am aware, however, of the significance within any tradition of the quality of the relationship between therapist and client, and this is an unknowable factor at present. I hope that we could establish a relationship that in itself (although inextricable from the core conditions) would have a positive effect in terms of Peta's self-regard. I hope that she would come to see herself as a wholly acceptable and valuable person, whose painful and difficult experiences do not in any way affect her intrinsic worth as a human being. I am aware that I currently see and would continue to see Peta in this light; that I like what I know of her; and that I have been very moved by some of the things she has said. At the same time, she may well simply not like me enough as a person to want to work with me.

Criteria for successful outcome

In so far as Peta typifies the state of discomfort and incongruence characteristic of clients at the outset of therapy, I hope that by its termination she would embody the characteristics of what Rogers describes as the 'fully functioning person'. She would be increasingly open to her own experiencing, able to allow her own positive and negative feelings without denial or distortion and to give appropriate expression to them. She would be able to live fully in the present, able to trust her own moment-by-moment responses as a guide to what is right for her. She would be less inclined to look outside herself for validation or guidance from external authority figures, and better able to form and sustain warm, close and nourishing relationships with others. She would be more likely to have a sense of personal freedom, able to take full responsibility for determining her own actions and able to experience herself as autonomous, not imprisoned by fate or circumstances (Thorne 1992: 34). In terms of Peta's own situation and presenting problem, this would mean that she would become less concerned to receive validation from men. Authority figures in general would be differently and less threateningly perceived. Hence she would be likely to be less attacking and thus to free herself from the painful negative cycle that she describes, where 'men I respect turn away from me so soon. Because they feel disempowered'. In feeling more autonomous and in charge of her own life, she would be freed from the 'learned defeatism' that holds her back in so many ways. I also hope that it would be possible for her to maintain her feminist understanding of the social construction of her own oppression as a woman without being held back in terms of her own organismic process by analysis and conceptualization.

I find it very interesting – and very promising – that Peta identifies her own lack of congruence as being at the heart of her discomfort in relationships, since Rogers identifies the client's increasing capacity for congruence as being of crucial significance in bringing about constructive personal change. Increased congruence, Rogers believes, enables the client to be more open to experience, more confident, more self-directing and empowered. It also means that the client can discriminate more accurately between those experiences which are enhancing and those which are destructive for her (Thorne 1992: 41).

I think that Peta has quite a reasonable chance of achieving Rogers' ideal of the 'fully functioning person', given a therapeutic relationship in which the core conditions are present, and given a willingness on her part to stay in that relationship until such a conclusion is reached. She has, as I have already indicated, considerable 'ripeness' for therapy and is either at or very near the edge of awareness on specific significant issues (e.g. her own incongruence). At the same time, she may choose to withdraw from the relationship at an earlier stage, perhaps even before the relationship is fully established, content to rest with 'modest gain in terms of the immediate crisis or situation that prompted entry to therapy' (Barrett-Lennard 1988: 13). Or she may choose to terminate once she has become clearer and less self-destructive in her relationships with men, yet perhaps with the deeper issues of self-worth and empowerment relatively unresolved.

I am wary of seeing 'success' in terms of the 'fully functioning person', because if I hold this ideal as a goal when I am working with a client, then I am likely to become impatient or frustrated whenever the client shows signs of not reaching that goal. It makes it more difficult to stay with the client exactly where she is in the here-and-now of the counselling relationship. It is also totally inconsistent with the approach that I am seeking to embody if I do anything other than accept Peta's decision to terminate at any point that feels right for her. It is *her* definition of 'success' that is of significance rather than any definition *I* might extract either from my experience with other clients, or from my understanding of person-centred theory.

Summary

As I read through Peta's original interview and her responses to my questions, I am aware of experiencing shifting and, on the whole, very positive feelings towards a woman who has had a difficult life in many respects, but who has not been defeated by circumstances. On the contrary, she is struggling through her difficulties towards further growth and self-understanding. Because it is impossible to predict the course of therapy in so far as, in terms of content, it is entirely client-directed, I cannot convey my own likely moment-by-moment responses, the flashes of warmth, sadness, irritation, affection that for me form the texture of the therapeutic relationship. It is as if what I have endeavoured to describe here is the outer shell of a potential relationship, without its heart. I have had to search for an intellectual understanding of Peta and the possibilities of her therapy, whereas our actual work together would very much depend on my suspension of such understanding. I have described what may emerge from being a companion to someone, without knowing what the reality of that companionship would involve. Nevertheless, I do have a sense that, while not without difficulties, a therapeutic relationship between us would work. I feel very engaged by Peta and optimistic about her capacity for constructive change within my particular therapeutic tradition.

Further reading

Barrett-Lennard, G.T. (1988). The pathway of client-centred therapy. Paper presented to the *First International Conference on Client-Centred and Experiential Psychotherapy*, University of Leuven.

Gendlin, E.T. (1982). *Focusing*. London: Bantam.

Mearns, D. and Thorne, B.J. (1988). *Person-Centred Counselling in Action*. London: Sage.

Rogers, C.J. (1951). *Client-Centered Therapy: Its Current Practice, Implications and Theory*. Boston, MA: Houghton Mifflin.

Rogers, C.J. (1961). *On Becoming a Person*. Boston, MA: Houghton Mifflin.

Temaner Brodley, B. (1993). The therapeutic clinical intervention – guidelines for beginning practice. In *Person Centred Practice*, Vol. I No. 2, pp. 15–21.

Thorne, B.J. (1992). *Carl Rogers*. London: Sage.

JOHN ORMROD

6

COGNITIVE BEHAVIOUR THERAPY

The therapist

Learning can often be a cyclical process. There are times when we both want and need a rigid framework from which to operate – a set of rules, guidelines or principles. There are, however, other times when growth and learning can only be achieved by a relaxation of this rigidity – time is needed to explore and play with new ideas, to branch out. We come full circle when this fresh learning is reintegrated into our personal framework; although hopefully our learning and growth is characterized by an upward spiral rather than a series of circles! Kelly (1955) coined the term 'creativity cycle' to describe this pattern.

I construe my therapeutic development in this light. Experiences as a psychology technician at a behavioural modification unit and my training as a clinical psychologist enthused me with the cognitive behavioural approach. With hindsight I am sure that my uncritical, total and at times dogmatic acceptance of these ideas was a defence against some of my anxieties. Confronted with new problems of enormous complexity, it was perhaps comforting to find therapies which were easily understandable (at least superficially) and which seemed to offer ready solutions.

My first appointment as a clinical psychologist was to a community mental health team. Fairly quickly I became somewhat disillusioned with cognitive behaviour therapy (CBT), or rather my understanding of it. I felt that it was too narrow. Thus, while regularly practising CBT, I began to develop an interest in insight-orientated and experiential psychotherapies.

Another influence on my therapeutic development has been a belief that debates about the relative merits of one therapy versus another have been somewhat sterile. There is a wealth of evidence arguing for the efficacy of psychological therapies (Luborsky *et al.* 1975), but despite enormous efforts there has been little to suggest from controlled group treatment trials that one therapy is superior to another (Smith and Glass 1977). Rather than disparage other therapeutic approaches, it strikes me as much more productive for therapists to attempt to find coherent ways of integrating diverse theoretical ideas in a way that also acknowledges the importance of their personality and that of their clients. I suspect that when I read the contributions of other therapists in this book, I will agree with almost everything they have said and will simply be left with a sense of frustration that I lacked the knowledge or imagination to include their insights into my way of working!

I would stress, however, that I do not advocate a shotgun approach to psychological therapy; more is required than just spraying the client with everything in the hope that something will work. Consistent with this stance, I am attracted to the ideas of Kelly, whose theory of personal construct psychology represents a framework for integration (Kelly 1955). Likewise, I see cognitive-analytic therapy (Ryle 1990) and Prochaska and DiClemente's (1982) transtheoretical model of change as useful models for achieving the sort of coherent eclecticism that I believe to be so important.

Recently, I have found that I have gone full circle, returning once again to CBT, although construing it in a broader manner as an integrative therapy. I share the cognitive model's conviction that identifying and disconfirming basic beliefs is important, but feel that this can be achieved through a variety of cognitive, behavioural, relationship or experiential techniques. Consistent with this view, Beck (1987) argues that the analysis of the format of such diverse therapies as psychoanalysis, behaviour therapy, Gestalt therapy and non-directive therapy suggests that the common factor for lasting change is the modification of core beliefs.

Finally, the cultural climate in which I work exerts a powerful influence. As an employee of the National Health Service (NHS), I am constantly confronted with the dilemma that demand outstrips potential supply. Every time somebody is seen for therapy, somebody else has been denied that opportunity. Not surprisingly, there are enormous pressures to target interventions towards the most psychologically disabled and to make such therapies as brief as possible. I feel sure these forces have had an impact on my therapeutic thinking and work. Ironically, in the context in which I work, it would be unlikely for Peta to receive psychological therapy.

Further information requested

Asking clients to complete a range of questionnaires prior to therapy is, for a number of reasons, part of my standard practice. They potentially elicit a vast amount of information. Background material can be collected which reduces the need for extensive history-taking. Therapists can be orientated to particularly significant areas in terms of what is said ('it was terrible being brought up in my family') or what is not said ('everything in my childhood was absolutely perfect'). Likewise, the style of completion reveals valuable information; for example, some questionnaires are typed in a clear methodical fashion, others have only the client's name filled in, and some are completed by spouses. The completion of questionnaires can also socialize people into the client role. Thus, as with therapy, answering questions can require considerable effort, it can often be painful and for many respondents it asks them to think about problems and issues in new ways. I would add that it is important to elicit clients' reactions to this task and to explain openly and clearly the function that they serve.

Peta was asked to complete the SCL-90-R (Derogatis 1983) and a Personal Background Information (PI) Questionnaire.

SCL-90-R

The SCL-90-R is a self-report inventory which asks respondents the extent to which they have been distressed or bothered during the last seven days by a range of ninety psychiatric symptoms. On three of the sub-scales, Peta scored at the 98th percentile relative to a normative sample. These were 'interpersonal sensitivity', which focuses on feelings of personal inadequacy and inferiority; 'paranoid ideation', which includes themes such as hostility, suspiciousness, grandiosity and fear of loss of autonomy; and 'psychoticism', which provides a graduated continuum from interpersonal alienation to evidence of psychosis. On one of the global indices which combines information on numbers of symptoms and intensity of perceived distress, Peta's score placed her at the 92nd percentile.

PI questionnaire

Originally designed as a structured interview, the PI questionnaire can now be administered in pen and paper form. The first two pages elicit basic demographic information. There follows a series of open questions, some of which are reported below together with most of Peta's responses.

What was it like for you, to grow up in your family?
Isolated. My brother arrived when I was nine. Until then I
had lived more or less alone with my mother. My father was
away at sea. I was bullied at school. Everyone thought I was
stupid. I must have been very withdrawn.

What have been important times, events or losses for your family?
Father's death in my mid-twenties. Grandmother's death a
few years before. Grandfather's death when my son was a
tiny baby. My son was born when I was 29. Abortion six
years ago. Divorce ten years ago. A miscarriage when my son
was three years old.

Please describe the nature of your difficulties. When did they start?
I feel that my childhood was spent in a kind of detached
dream world, mostly, but not wholly, to do with being
profoundly bored at school and being bullied.
   I relate to men differently from women. I mostly feel that
men are a puzzle to me: I experience men as defensive. They
may experience me as a threat.
   At forty-five, I feel that I am a threat to other women
because I am unattached, but must never show my needs. I
must conceal myself because it is inappropriate for a women
of my age to show her sexuality. Certainly this is true in the
job I do and at home.

What sense, if any, do you make of them?
I mostly have to adjust to the situation whether I like it or
not. I read a lot. All through my childhood books were a
refuge – the only thing available really.

What has happened that leads you to seek help now?
Loneliness. A sense of isolation. A constant feeling that I am
difficult for some people, some men perhaps. Last summer I
had a huge row with a man . . . (his anger) was really
frightening.

In what ways do you hope seeing a therapist will help you?
Insight does come in this kind of work. I am really interested
in what may be revealed.

Do you have any worries about seeing a therapist?
Some, not enough to halt or inhibit my decision. I do feel
vulnerable and hope that I would feel I could trust a
therapist to intuitively know when I was hurt.

Have you ever had any form of professional help for your problems (e.g. from a counsellor, GP or psychiatrist)? If so, please give details.
  Yes, ten years ago. He was primarily person-centred. I loved him. He was great.

The interviewer was asked to explore a number of specific areas in more detail with Peta. For some of these Peta was asked to remember when she had first felt like this, and asked whether there were particular thoughts or images associated with how she felt. Other issues were explored along the lines of 'can you tell me more about . . . ?'.

Problems with authority figures
  That's really interesting. I was at nursery school. I got taken to nursery school and then dumped in a place *without having been consulted.*
  To obey . . . seems ridiculous to me, in some curious way. My womanly self [*exhaled deeply*] . . . obey? No chance, absolutely no chance.
  My whole schooling was a total waste of time. And teachers have power and authority and I learned to acquiesce and be obedient . . . most of the time . . . but I think it accounts for a great deal of rage. I have always relished and needed my heroes.

Feelings of being rejected
  [Talking about recent experience of good man friend curtailing some time they had together to go for a drink with another person] . . . I am no good. I am not worthy of attention . . . the attention of this one person, I am not worthy or in some way do not come up to – you know how the particular is generalized. And . . . it's connected with being labelled as backward. If I'm not acceptable then you internalize the messages. You become not acceptable. [*Pauses*] And it hurts really. Lots of sorrow.

Conditioning as a woman
  The most significant conditioning came from my mother. Girls must not make themselves sexually available. Men are not to be trusted sexually. They have uncontrollable urges. So women have a kind of power but it isn't a power to be proactive. Something fearful and scary and all that stuff. The only life choices that were open to me as a woman were

nursing and teaching and secretarial work. I didn't want to be any of those things actually. But the problem was I didn't know what I wanted to be . . . Certain things were acceptable. Other things were completely unknown and therefore terribly dangerous.

And I'm learning more and more in my later life, to own important life decisions for myself – not even to discuss it with other people. I got myself to art college. I did that, and I didn't talk about it to anyone. I just knew if this didn't come right then I really was truly lost.

Being bullied

It's a kind of key again, and has a lot of power behind it. Emotional power. It was so easy to bully me. There was no way I could communicate my experience of school and of being bullied at school . . . because I must have . . . um . . . had such a strong feeling that I . . . that nothing would be done. I became a victim. I didn't speak with the same accent. I didn't share any of the norms and values in a sort of sociological way. If I had a rubber that somebody wanted to borrow, and for some reason I chose not to lend it . . . I was called a Jew – and I *was* a Jew.

Can you tell me a little more about your father's death?

The circumstances of his death and how I was at that time in history are quite painful to me. I was angry and hurt and alone, not able to communicate these feelings. My relationship with my mother was not good either really, it was horrible, and I'm ashamed of that time, that he should have died . . . that he wouldn't go to the doctor. Everyone knew he was ill; he refused to accept it, absolute denial. He feared that if he went to the doctor he would learn something about the extent of his ill health and he didn't want to do that. He wanted to die suddenly. He told me he was ill. He probably had several minor heart attacks. I should have taken him by the scruff of the neck and said, 'You're going to the doctor now, and I'm taking you and that's the way it's going to be'. Sorrow that he didn't see my *son*. It's good to talk about. I haven't talked about it . . . I haven't talked about this at all. I've been wanting to for ages. I can't talk about it with anyone.

I can't ever remember having had a conversation with my father. And maybe that's not true but I *feel* it.

Can you tell me a little more about the power struggle between you and your brother and how it included your father?
My father and brother used to play-fight and this has a lot of significance for me because I was a bystander. I couldn't join in. I was excluded. And I used to watch them and despair having so much loving fun, and I was too old; I'd lost out. That's a really big thing. To feel that kind of jealousy. It was feeling excluded from the male world which I think has important connections to the present.

Has anyone abused you in the past?
When I was about eight or nine. No, the answer is strictly no. There was a tiny little episode. My parents were on the boat at the time, because I was brought up on a boat until I was eleven. I'm sure I was impossible; and flew into a fury and sent to my room. And I was taken there forcefully because I was totally freaking out . . . having a major tantrum, and I was held down by my father. Actually what I wanted to do was to communicate. But abuse is funny, because sometimes we can feel bloody abused by neglect. So when someone says, 'Was there abuse?', I say, 'I don't know'. But 'no' is strictly right.

Can you tell me a little more about your discomfort telling me in the first session that you are a feminist?
It isn't comfortable being a feminist. I don't want to go through my life alienating people and I know some men are terribly – they're made uncomfortable . . . and my instinct is to draw back, almost physically, if I'm having that effect.

Assessment

'There's nothing either good or bad but thinking makes it so' (Hamlet to Rosencrantz).
Cognitive therapy is based on an underlying theoretical rationale that an individual's affect and behaviour are largely determined by the way in which he or she structures the world (Beck 1976). Part of the assessment process therefore entails attempting to trace the links between a person's thoughts, feelings and behaviours. Full use is made of the interaction between client and therapist to develop further understanding. There is rarely a more valuable source of information about the beliefs from which a person is operating from than that derived from exploration of the therapeutic relationship.

Clearly, there is a fundamental difference between reading a transcript and being with somebody as they relate the same story. Thus my attempts at understanding some of the material Peta has presented within a CBT framework are presented in an extremely tentative fashion.

There is a large body of evidence which suggests that early relationships particularly those with family members result in the development of a set of basic ideas, beliefs and expectations about the self, others and patterns of interaction (Safran and Segal 1990). Peta talks extensively about her fear of men and her anger and puzzlement towards them. These themes seem to have been present from an early age, arising initially out of her relationship with her parents. Later, social relationships feed the self-concept, and it is through our interaction with the social environment that our sense of self is built up (Brown and Harris 1978). Some of Peta's adult relationships, for example with her husband, may have reinforced some of her early beliefs. Intertwined with various life events has been her commitment to feminism. Withdrawing ('into a dream world') seems to have been one way that Peta dealt with early trauma. In later years, I wonder whether she also learnt to protect herself by going on the attack. This could be conceptualized as 'attack them before they attack me' or 'defence is the best form of attack'. These thoughts are outlined in Fig. 4. Clearly our environment does not simply impinge on us but rather we actually help to shape it. Thus the suspiciousness of the paranoid person, for example, may result in other people withdrawing and avoiding them, thereby confirming their basic beliefs about the hostility of others. In Peta's diagram, I have speculated as to whether her current ways of coping actually increase her puzzlement and anger towards men.

Interestingly, Peta seems to feel that to attract men (perhaps in part a legacy of her mother's influence) she has to become acquiescent or submissive. I imagine that this in turn leads her at times to feel frustrated and also contradicts her feminist views. It is almost as though she acts in accordance with the belief, 'a strong, confident and assertive woman cannot be in a relationship with a man'. I wonder whether, in addition, she finds it difficult reconciling her feminist beliefs and her desires for intimacy with men.

Another factor in her difficulties with men might again relate to her early experiences with her father. Denied a close, loving relationship with him, she perhaps in turn attempts to compensate by idolizing certain male figures (Peta talks about her love for a previous counsellor and the importance of heroes), which ultimately leads to disappointment as reality dawns in long-term adult relationships. Possibly related to this are Peta's career aspirations – she wants to

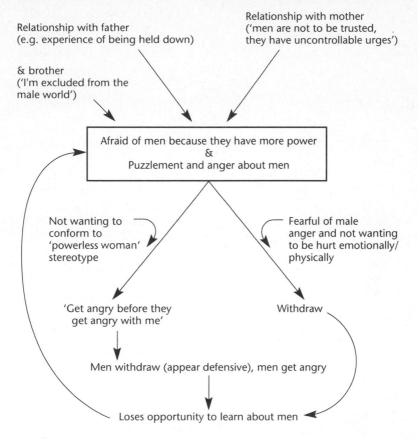

Relationship with father
(e.g. experience of being held down)

Relationship with mother
('men are not to be trusted,
they have uncontrollable urges')

& brother
('I'm excluded from the
male world')

Afraid of men because they have more power
&
Puzzlement and anger about men

Not wanting to
conform to
'powerless woman'
stereotype

Fearful of male
anger and not wanting
to be hurt emotionally/
physically

'Get angry before they
get angry with me'

Withdraw

Men withdraw (appear defensive), men get angry

Loses opportunity to learn about men

Figure 4

work in a small team – again perhaps an unconscious attempt to experience something, in this instance family life, largely denied to her as a child.

One way Peta as a small child could have made sense of her father's rejecting behaviour was perhaps to conclude 'I'm not acceptable'. This hypothesis is depicted in Fig. 5, together with guesses about its possible impact on relationships and the anxieties she expresses about applying for jobs.

My sense from reading Peta's interviews is that she would be a skilled intuiter. I wonder though whether at times she perhaps places too much emphasis on this style of processing. Thus she seemed very confident that a friend knew instantaneously what she had

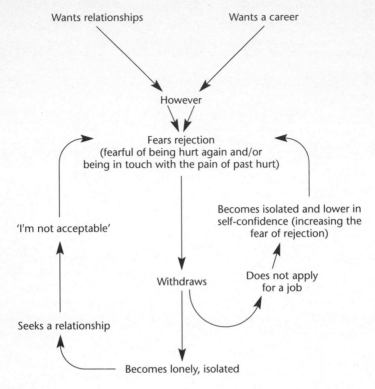

Figure 5

been thinking and I was struck by her hope that a therapist 'would instinctively know when I was hurt'. Clearly, there are risks attached to drawing firm conclusions from inadequate information, especially when they confirm an erroneous view of the world.

In Fig. 6, I have highlighted the chain of thinking Peta identified when a friend curtailed a chat with her. It is noteworthy because it highlights some theoretical aspects of cognitive therapy. Following this perceived rebuff, her thoughts generalize to damning self statements which she relates to the internalized message from childhood that she is 'not acceptable'. Such thoughts, according to the cognitive model, would have an impact on how she felt and once mood had been influenced in this way her thinking and processing of information would be likely to intensify this feeling, thereby creating a vicious circle.

From her questionnaire response, it is evident that Peta has experienced a number of losses (grandmother's death, father's death,

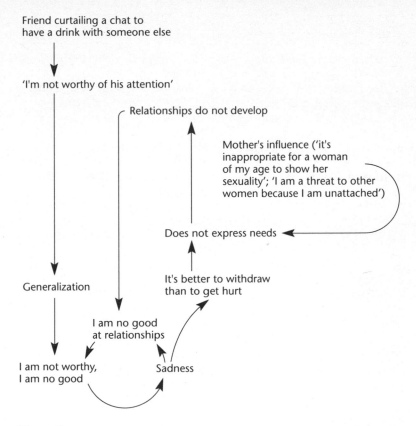

Figure 6

grandfather's death, miscarriage, divorce, an abortion) in what would appear to be a relatively short period of time. With regard to her father's death, she acknowledges that she has not spoken about it and also that this is something she needs to do. Perhaps her strategy for dealing with emotional pain (to withdraw?) has not facilitated the grieving process and this, coupled with her guilt about her father's death, may have made these losses all the more frightening and difficult to resolve.

Therapeutic possibilities (and problem areas)

I have chosen to look at these areas together, because in many instances a possibility has inherent problems, just as problems can often be reconstrued as opportunities.

Opportunities	Difficulties
To experience a good role model of a man who will not neglect, and who is open and receptive to her feelings, especially those of anger	Stereotypes held by the therapist, e.g. (1) women should not be angry (2) limited expectations of women
Immediately throws up a key issue, i.e. how she relates to men and offers the chance to work on this in a safe environment	Failure to achieve a balance between recognizing the impact of socio-economic and political factors and acknowledging the importance of an individual's life history ('it's all society's fault' *vs* 'it's all to do with you')
Ending – if handled well, offers an opportunity to look at previous endings, to see how present one could be different, to acknowledge sad feelings, but also to value the sense of moving on and progress that has been made	Ending – if issues of termination are not handled sensitively, there could be potential problems, e.g. (1) possible reaffirmation of Peta's belief that men will always withdraw if she expresses strong feelings (2) damaging re-enactment of relationship with father

Figure 7

Peta's prime areas of concern revolve around her feminist views and anger, fearfulness and puzzlement towards men. Gender issues will be crucial to therapy (Walker 1990). In Fig. 7, I have outlined some of the potential opportunities and difficulties inherent in Peta seeing a male therapist. I would imagine that a similar table could be drawn up were Peta to see a female therapist. The therapeutic challenge is to ensure that the 'gender agenda' stays to the fore in therapy and I would anticipate that Peta would be a good ally in achieving this goal.

I think that there are aspects of CBT that maximize the likelihood of exploiting the opportunities and minimizing the difficulties outlined above. CBT should be open and collaborative in its style, and as such can be empowering for a client. Assessment thoughts are typically shared and shaped by joint discussion between therapist and client. Just as Peta brought her spider diagram to the assessment interview, I might want to share with her my assessment diagrams to explore with her their validity and to make the necessary corrections and additions. I would add, however, some suggestions about ways of escaping from some of the vicious circles that I have hypothesized. Simply giving someone a sheet outlining their 'stuckness' is unlikely to be particularly helpful.

Another aspect of the therapeutic style which I feel potentially offers Peta certain advantages is its emphasis on experimentation and working on any anxieties which impede this process. Part of my thinking about Peta is that doing things differently feels very risky (she says, 'other things were completely unknown and therefore terribly dangerous', and later when talking about her decision to go to art college, 'I just knew that if this didn't come right, then I really was truly lost'). This fear perhaps stops her trying out new ways of being, leaving her with a limited range of options in certain situations and problem areas.

There are particular aspects of how Peta seems to relate (especially to men) to which the therapist will need to be especially sensitive. I have speculated that Peta perhaps idolizes certain men (compensating for early loss?) and then is perhaps left disappointed when they do not live up to expectations. She also seems to withdraw when confronted with emotional pain and believes that expressing her anger and her feminist views drives men away. Although these hypothesized aspects of her personal style are potentially problematic for therapy, careful monitoring of the therapeutic process (ideally by both parties) will give the opportunity to observe them happening in the here and now, and make discovering the beliefs that underpin these behaviours an easier and a more meaningful process, which will in turn hopefully facilitate therapeutic work.

When asked in the PI questionnaire if she has any worries about seeing a therapist, Peta talks about her feelings of vulnerability and a hope that her therapist would intuitively know when she was hurt. Again I think CBT offers a framework for talking about these issues openly at the outset of therapy. I would, for example, point out the risks attached to believing or expecting that a therapist can reliably intuit feelings. The immediate therapeutic issue might be to understand more about what makes the explicit communication of feelings potentially difficult for Peta in this situation.

The course of therapy

Cognitive behaviour therapy is a collective term which includes a variety of theoretical positions and therapeutic styles. Sometimes it is characterized as a somewhat cold intellectual pursuit aimed at changing or (worse still!) challenging people's thinking. Alternatively, it is described as nothing more than positive thinking, looking on the bright side and ignoring social, economic and political realities. However, CBT also subsumes approaches which place great emphasis on the therapeutic relationship, whose style is collaborative and which attempt to help people:

- to develop insight into the beliefs that influence their behaviour,
- to learn to treat beliefs as hypotheses and to test out ideas,
- to design experiments aimed at identifying other ways of construing the world and the self, and
- to develop new skills.

From such a theoretical position, the actual therapeutic techniques employed can be many and varied, borrowing from almost any other tradition. Many writers have cautioned against the tyranny of technique. Clients are not a set of disconnected problems to which one can apply techniques *ad hoc*. Techniques need to be crafted into the therapeutic relationship, in which the therapist qualities of accurate empathy, positive regard and genuineness are of prime import. Indeed, in some instances, the therapeutic relationship can be the most important source for developing new ideas about the self. By empathizing and listening, a therapist can enable the client to experience a helpful and accepting relationship; and in this way the client may internalize greater self-acceptance, via the acceptance and understanding of the therapist.

In the early stages of therapy with Peta, I would be keen to establish a good therapeutic relationship, to socialize her into the therapeutic milieu, to explain the model and to identify goals. Not surprisingly, people are often anxious about entering therapy and may have misapprehensions about what might be involved in CBT. It can be useful to talk about what therapy might entail; perhaps emphasizing that CBT is active and structured in nature, frequently making use of agendas to plan each session, and that considerable importance is attached to homework assignments. Although there is this emphasis on structure, I would not want to take this to an extreme. Clearly, one needs to be sensitive to the current state of a client. If Peta wanted to share some painful feelings which fell outside an agreed agenda, little would be gained in trying to do highly focused work. Indeed, given Peta's early experiences, ignoring her feelings in such a way is likely to be a damaging repetition of past trauma. Whereas the converse, active listening and empathic responding, might offer the opportunity for new learning in terms of how she construes men.

It might be appropriate at this stage to agree a therapeutic contract. CBT is typically a time-limited therapy. Although again an item for some discussion, I could anticipate Peta and I meeting weekly for about twenty sessions. Given the experiences of loss that she alludes to in the PI questionnaire, I would be less willing than normal to agree to 'booster sessions' and 'follow-ups', in the belief that a clear ending might facilitate the resolution of termination issues.

In explaining the therapeutic model to Peta, I might well utilize a standard example such as that of Gilbert (1992). Peta could be asked to imagine a person hearing a sound in their kitchen at 2 a.m. and to write down that person's possible emotional responses and the beliefs that might underpin these:

Sound in the kitchen	It may be a thief	Anxiety/fear
	It is my drunken husband who has forgotten his key	Anger
	It is my cat	Calm
	It is my child home safely after a party	Relief

Two other areas, namely context and history, would also need to be discussed. Clearly, if one does not have a child this cannot be part of the evaluation. Second, if someone has been abused, then anxiety might become terror due to the activation of memory.

I might then want to explore an example from her own experience using thoughts and feelings that arise during therapy or from historic material such as that outlined in Fig. 5. Between sessions, Peta might find that some form of self-monitoring of her thoughts, feelings and behaviour (e.g. keeping a diary) might be useful. In the PI questionnaire, Peta mentions her enthusiasm for reading and at this point I might offer to lend her some reading on CBT so that she could become more informed about this way of working.

Role-play can be a powerful technique for eliciting various forms of meaning and is a useful way of invoking affect and demonstrating the influence of thoughts on mood. For example, in the therapy session, Peta might be asked to re-enact a previous painful event, such as an argument with a man, noting her thoughts and feelings as she does this. Another method for increasing the awareness of the internal self-dialogue and its emotive effects is the two chairs technique (Safran and Segal 1990).

During the course of therapy, I would be particularly interested in discovering Peta's core beliefs; ideas related to the pursuit of long-term goals, rules for living, idealizations, hopes and fears, and beliefs about self and significant others. In Fig. 5, 'I am not worthy' is perhaps illustrative of such a core belief. When active, such thoughts can exert a major influence in terms of how the world is construed and are thus a key therapeutic focus. Sometimes in therapy the presence of strong feelings indicates that a core belief has been exposed. As with other therapies, this affective experience is considered important as insight into key ideas and their possible change often depends on a certain level of emotional response. When Peta talked about her friend shortening their time together to go for a drink with another person, it seemed that she quickly began to experience strong feelings of hurt and sorrow. These were perhaps related to the belief 'I am not worthy', which in turn might have stemmed from her relationship with her father. Thus for Peta a specific situation gave rise to a chain of inferences in her head resulting in feelings of great distress. Helping develop insight into such chains is one of the therapeutic goals of CBT.

One method for identifying Peta's major assumptions might be to use an imagery technique. The therapist asks the client to close her eyes and picture the earliest memory she has of a distressing experience as similar as possible to the one she is undergoing. If such an event is recalled, the client is asked to state in one sentence the underlying belief that she was operating from at that time, and how at the time she coped with the experience. When Peta was asked to think about difficulties with authority figures, she recalled an early instance of being dumped at nursery school. At that developmental stage, her range of coping options would have been limited. Clearly, Peta felt angry at her treatment but perhaps could only deal with the situation by withdrawing. It might then be productive to focus on the advantages and disadvantages of this coping behaviour currently, while at the same time recognizing that in the past it may have been adaptive.

Later in therapy there might be instances in which Peta finds it useful to target specific thoughts for change. Looking for evidence and generating alternatives for specific thoughts might help this. Some clients, for example, find it useful to note down their depressing or anxiety-inducing thoughts, and to try to come up with alternative ways of construing an event. An addition to this exercise might be to note down the past experience that contributes to the initial thought. An example for Peta might look like this:

Current belief	Contributing past experience	Alternative
I'm not acceptable	Relationship with father	Although as a child I inferred from my father's behaviour that I wasn't acceptable, as an adult I now know this was more to do with him than me. I have several adult friendships in which I am accepted

Another method with which to investigate the validity of a specific assumption consists of designing an experiment or task to test out the idea empirically. Should it be confirmed in therapy, for example, that Peta believes she can never express anger towards a man without negative consequences, a homework task could be devised to test this out with Peta, noting what happens in terms of her thoughts and feelings and the behaviour of others.

Throughout therapy, I would want to ensure that the themes of loss and Peta's feminist perspective are not lost. It might be that as therapy is ending, issues of separation and loss become particularly salient and the termination of therapy might offer a valuable opportunity to address such areas.

Criteria for successful outcome

Part of the process of therapy would have been to agree therapeutic goals and to have monitored progress towards their achievement. Typically, this would be done informally, although on occasions it might be achieved in a more structured fashion by using rating sheets consisting of a series of visual analogue scales, one for each agreed target. The mid-point of each scale could represent for Peta her condition at the outset of therapy with the two extremes representing 'aim achieved' and 'worst state possible'. At the start of each therapy session Peta could be asked to reflect on how things were currently and to rate this on the sheets. Such a procedure can help to ensure therapy remains focused, encourage frequent reviews of the therapeutic process and may reinforce the idea that the aim of therapy is to work on, and hopefully achieve, a set of explicit goals (Ryle, 1990). Such ratings, of course, are by no means an objective measure and will be subject to bias.

In addition to such individual ratings, I would want to re-administer the SCL-90-R. Certainly, some clients are keen to review changes in their symptom levels pre- and post-therapy, but in addition it is part of a routine effort to monitor the impact of psychological therapy with all clients. Again it is recognized that such an instrument is not a pure measure of therapeutic change, nor in any way does its administration reflect a belief that the sole determinant of successful therapy is a reduction in reported symptoms.

In a more general sense, I would hope that our work together had succeeded in recognizing the impact of societal and individual factors in her difficulties, and that Peta had satisfied her aim, at least in part, of developing insight both at an intellectual and affective level.

Summary

In conclusion, it seems important to reiterate two fundamental aspects of CBT:

1 *Its style is open and collaborative.* Although I have outlined my assessment thoughts and matched certain therapeutic techniques to these, this does not necessarily reflect how CBT should be conducted. CBT should not be a 'recipe book' approach to therapy, matching routine procedures to certain 'maladaptive' thinking styles. Rather, it is a process of joint exploration with a client, with an emphasis on clarifying and reviewing material that is discussed to arrive at a shared understanding. Specific therapeutic 'tasks' are selected in a similar fashion.

2 *CBT offers a framework for integration.* By choosing to concentrate on certain areas and possible ways of working, I have obviously neglected other aspects which may be of equal or greater importance. Given the potential breadth of CBT, such omissions are more likely to reflect personal limitations rather than limits imposed by this particular therapeutic model.

Further reading

Beck, A.T. (1976). *Cognitive Therapy and the Emotional Disorders.* New York: International Universities Press.

Beck, A.T. (1987). Cognitive therapy. In J.K. Zeig (Ed.), *The Evolution of Psychotherapy.* New York: Bruner Mazel.

Brown, G.W. and Harris, T. (1978). *The Social Origins of Depression.* London: Tavistock.

Derogatis, L.R. (1983). *SCL-90-R Administration, Scoring and Procedures Manual – II.* Towson: Clinical Psychometric Research.

Gilbert, P. (1992) *Counselling for Depression.* London: Sage.

Kelly, G.A. (1955). *The Psychology of Personal Constructs*. New York: W.W. Norton.

Luborsky, L., Singer, B. and Luborsky, L. (1975). Comparative studies of psychotherapies. *Archives of General Psychiatry*, Vol. 32, pp. 995–1008.

Prochaska, J.O. and DiClemente, C.C. (1982). Transtheoretical therapy: Toward a more integrative model of change. *Psychotherapy: Theory, Research and Practice*, vol. 3, pp. 276–88.

Ryle, A. (1990). *Cognitive Analytic Therapy: Active Participation in Change*. Chichester: John Wiley.

Safran, J.D. and Segal, Z.V. (1990). *Interpersonal Processes in Cognitive Therapy*. New York: Basic Books.

Smith, M.I. and Glass, G.V. (1977). Meta-analysis of psychotherapy outcome studies. *American Psychologist*, Vol. 32, pp. 752–60.

Walker, M. (1990). *Women in Therapy and Counselling*. Buckingham: Open University Press.

JOHN ROWAN

HUMANISTIC AND INTEGRATIVE PSYCHOTHERAPY

The therapist

When I came into this area I was a social psychologist, working in the field of social and consumer research. I learned about psychotherapy in the turbulent days of the early 1970s, mainly through humanistic groupwork. As we all did in those days, before the existence of any kind of relevant training courses, I apprenticed myself to several different group leaders (Will Schutz, Jay Stattmen, Jim Elliott), and learned a great deal from each of them. I started leading my own groups in 1972. On the theoretical side, I got very involved with the Association for Humanistic Psychology and eventually wrote a book entitled *Ordinary Ecstasy* (Rowan 1976), summarizing what I had learned up to that point. At the same time, I was getting into the anti-sexist men's movement, and later wrote a book on feminism from a male standpoint (Rowan 1987). This is really what made me interested in the person at the centre of this book, after refusing the chance to work with a different client. Peta somehow rang a bell with me.

Then I discovered co-counselling, and became more interested in one-to-one work. I became a teacher of the approach known as the Barefoot Psychoanalyst. I also took a qualification in applied behavioural science, and started to do a good deal of work with organizations. This ended with my heading up the Behavioural Science Unit in the Greater London Council.

The turning point came about 1978–80. During that period, I moved much more into one-to-one psychotherapy, taking a qualification in primal integration with Dr William Swartley. I also got involved in setting up the Institute for Psychotherapy and Social Studies with Dr Giora Doron. This brought me into close contact with colleagues who were psychoanalytically oriented, and I learned a great deal about psychoanalysis from this involvement. When I came to write my chapter entitled 'Primal Integration' (Rowan 1988), I found that this psychoanalytic understanding fitted in very well and helped to make the theory more explicit. In my later book on *Subpersonalities* (Rowan 1990), I was able to outline a developmental model which integrated the work of Freud, Winnicott, Janov, Assagioli and others. This actually fits well with Peta, as we shall see later.

In 1980, I helped to found the Association for Humanistic Psychology Practitioners, which was and is concerned with questions of accreditation, ethics and standards in the whole area of humanistic psychology and its ramifications, including the question of equal opportunities.

From all this came my practice, which I outlined in a book entitled *The Reality Game* (Rowan 1983). It is a holistic approach to psychotherapy, paying attention to the client's intellect, feelings, body and soul. I believe in the whole person; that is, that the client exists on several different levels, and that I have to pay attention to all those levels if I want to do justice to the person.

As a therapist, I think I am quite nosy, quite intrusive, quite curious to understand everything. I tend not to let things slip by without questioning them. If some possibility occurs to me, I will usually check it out with the client, rather than holding back on it. I tend to work with the client, rather than standing back and observing the client. With this particular client, I believe my grounding in feminism helped me to understand where she was coming from, and to have a feeling for what would be relevant to her.

Further information requested

I asked for more information about her brother. It seemed to me that a good deal of the energy was centred on him.
She answered in a curious way, as if she had no real memory of her early childhood. She evidently went to her photograph album to check up. One of the photographs is very revealing. It shows the mother and the baby brother. The mother is holding the baby on her lap and looking fondly down at it, and the baby is regarding the camera. To one side of the picture is the father, sitting on a step which seems to lead out of the room. He is focused on the baby, though his near arm is pointing away from the couple. His right arm, further away from the couple, is being leaned over by the face of Peta, who is sitting next to, but slightly behind, him. So she is looking round him, and is also smiling at the baby.

Family photographs are almost always revealing, and this one shows pretty clearly the way in which the family hero was the baby at this point in time. But her own words about this are:

> I guess it would take some time to unearth that material. I'm not sure. I could probably do that with your help [*said to M.W.*], because you're skilled and experienced in the psychodynamic traditions and I – that would be the only way I could access it.

It seems clear from all this that there are things about her early relationship with her brother that she does not want to remember.

I asked about her relationship with her father.
According to Peta, he was 'stunningly good-looking'. It seems that when her mother rejected her in favour of her brother she turned to her father. But he did not respond in any very helpful way. She says of the photograph that her father was called down to be in the photo:

> He was ill at ease physically, because basically he was shy and introverted and didn't really want to show it – and put a sweater on and came and sat down, and he had this little girl kid, you know, snuggling up against this vast man person, and both of them thinking actually, 'What the hell'.
>
> [She had a memory of her father]: We are in his workshop (he always had workshops which were away from the home, separate, entirely his domain, visited infrequently by few). He is building something out of wood. I want to help. I am about eight. I take some tools in my hands. I want to be part of something. He hates this. I can feel he transmits to me a kind of loathing. I feel it in my whole self, whole body. It feels like self-disgust. Diseased. I can't use the tools, they are too big and heavy. He barely restrains his impatience. I leave.
>
> [Later she says]: I remember struggling to manage my solitude. It's even tight in my ... [*points to her chest*] you know. There's a quality of hopelessness that settles over a kid when they know that you can't damn well get through to an adult, because they don't have the power ... he was certainly not available. [And she also says]: He couldn't connect and I couldn't connect, and there wasn't anybody else. And the terror of it, just blew me off – so there wasn't anywhere else except to be by myself. [She quotes a poem which she found and collected in her youth, by Yevgeny Yevtushenko]:

... Solitude can embrace
As a man cannot embrace
But the dress is worn on bare
Nerves
and all its hooks are red-hot!
'I love being alone!' is to shout
'It doesn't hurt' under torture.
But it does hurt,
Lord how it hurts ...

That seems to capture some of her mood. It seems clear that she was desperately lonely some of the time. Her feelings about her father are terribly ambivalent – wanting him so much, but also disappointed in him for being interested in things rather than in people.

I said that she seemed to give men a lot of power.
I don't give it. They have it. [They *take* it?] When I wish so devoutly for equality they defend. If my brother decides he has nothing to say, what can I do? He's over six feet tall and has physically dominated me for years. I'm scared. He *has* more power. (Powerlessness feels like drowning. Chest constricts. Guts are taut, ready for flight. Breath gets shallow. I become very still in an attempt to become invisible. Like being bullied at school. If I can just become smaller. I'm not here really.) Yes, scenes from the past come back but I can't write about them.

This is the first mention of fear, and may be a clue to why she is so reluctant to remember her early days with her brother. It may be not just a fear of being hurt, but a terror of non-being, annihilation.

I asked about her relationship with her mother.
I think my mother has actually poisoned – that's a terribly strong word ... she ... her body is absolutely racked with cancer – she's been a chronic asthmatic all her life. She was persecuted as a child, she didn't know her parents, just awful ... she hated and feared men on the whole – or the power that they potentially – they did have a lot of power over her life, fundamentally at a horribly deep level. They screwed her up really, and she never has come to that completeness we would wish for all women to have. And I ... maybe I won't go into that but I know that she has absolutely had a dire effect on ... her sharp cruel judgements, and assumptions, and not being able to separate what's mine from hers, and all ...

She was and still is highly articulate, extremely diligent in whatever project she gets into. Art history. The history of thought. A lot of existential ponderings at the moment. She's now seventy.

Why did they marry? He had been married before briefly, in the States. She told me this long after he died. It was supposed to be a family secret. There's another family secret: they were going to abort me when mum discovered she was pregnant. Penniless in Brooklyn, New York City, both communists. He was ten years older. Looking at the photographs now, photographs of my father holding me as a baby, I feel perhaps a little of what my mother must have felt when she 'fell in love with' my father.

There is some dramatic stuff here, again not quite spelt out, some of it hidden from awareness.

I asked her about silence, and what it brought to mind.
My father. He doesn't have any words. She has them all. (Phew!) But I need him to speak. He never does. Maybe I just forget. I can't get anything else here. I'm remembering the feeling, though. It hurts, like something in the core of me is thwarted. Tight. Blocked. (Because I remember so little – this dissociation is bothering me. Obviously I don't want to remember.) And now I live alone.

So silence on her own is bearable, but silence in the presence of another person is horrible.

I asked about her son.
Of course I have got it wrong with my son. And the consequences are that he will remain angry with me for a long time. It would have been impossible to get it right. Because the wrongness is because I have been a single mother trying to raise her only son. Sometimes I can sense the same anger in my son as in my brother: they both experience me as controlling, domineering, confident. Also, when they are together they collude and shut out my mother and myself. The two old women. I'm quite sure they feel shut out by 'us'. God what a mess.

I know he loves me. I know that I love him.

This again speaks volumes about the difficulty of a mother raising a son in our culture, and with her particular early experiences.

All this additional information helped me a great deal. I felt quite honoured and humble to have been given so much.

Assessment

It seems fairly obvious that Peta had a painful childhood after her brother was born. That comes out very clearly from the answers given. What is not at all clear is what happened in the years before her brother was born. This seems very important, in the light of all the answers we have now showing the high emotional level associated with trying to remember these early years.

My discipline encourages me to go back a long way, and not to make too many rules about what can be remembered and what cannot. If we go back to her womb life, it seems that this must have been fraught with anxiety. Her mother would have been a young wife, not perhaps sure yet of her position (as a second wife), short of money, unsure of the future, an outsider who had considered abortion. If, as Frank Lake (1980) says, 'The foetus is marinated in the mother's feelings', this was a tension-filled womb to be held in. We know nothing about the birth – I wish I had asked about this – but in all probability it would have been mechanical, impersonal and unsympathetic. And then what welcome greeted the newcomer?

The father would not have been around very much; he was often absent, and even when he was physically present it does not seem that he would ever have been able to have warm or close relationships with anyone. In an essay on gender, Peta quotes some statements which seem to me to resonate strongly with her own experience:

> From the little girl's point of view, Daddy is a mystery, a powerful figure who is always leaving. She has no power to keep him there or to get the attention she wants from him . . . He does not rescue her from the difficult aspects of her relationship with mother. He does not want to see her needy and wanting part. He does not offer her a real alternative.
> (Eichenbaum and Orbach 1984: 55)

The essay goes on about the father being unaware of – uninterested in – the child's point of view. And we get another powerful quote: 'He is encouraged in a kind of moral laziness which stunts his growth: his capacities for empathetic generosity atrophy through disuse' (Dinnerstein 1987). It seems to me that these quotes speak very particularly to Peta, and that they refer directly to her experience of her own father. The second quote, in fact, is also used in a quite different essay written on another occasion. It must have stuck in her memory.

As for the mother, Peta says, 'She raised me in a very loving way, which is why I'm a loving person . . . '. This suggests that there was a welcome there. So perhaps relations with the mother were 'normal' for the first few years. But I am not sure about this. Peta says:

> I didn't think of myself as having been a girl really. (This is up to puberty. Before puberty.) I didn't talk the way girls did at school. I certainly didn't dress like a girl much when I was at home on the boat. I didn't do girlish things apparently. At home I had a dinghy (a house-dwellers bike) and rowed about the creek (mostly alone) where the boat was moored.

This suggests that she did not identify with her mother even in the earlier years. So was the mother really 'very loving' in the way suggested? All the indications seem to be that Peta identified with her father much more, even before the brother was born. Could it even be that the mother turned to the brother in part because she could not relate at all satisfactorily to her daughter?

These are difficult questions, and they arise only because Peta is so obviously reluctant to remember anything that happened before the baby was born. It is perhaps as if the baby's arrival, and all that is connected with that, were a 'screen memory' in the Freudian sense – that is, a memory which is accurately and importantly remembered, and which masks anything earlier and perhaps more traumatic. Peta can't remember, and perhaps won't remember, anything earlier. I asked her what was her first memory, and she replied, 'Because of the nature of what I do know about my childhood there are huge bits that I don't remember'. That is really quite a curious answer, because it completely avoids answering the question. At another point she says, 'I don't know what my first memory is. Why should such a straightforward question make me feel so miserable? I am deprived of my own history. (More sick, sad feelings, make another cigarette.)' This does again point to some kind of 'body' being 'buried' in the earlier period of time.

All the evidence seems to me consistent with the possibility that the set-up which is blamed on the coming of the brother – an inability to relate either to the mother or to the father – may have existed much earlier, and perhaps right from the start. Perhaps she never really trusted her mother, and perhaps she always had an unrequited love for her father.

The coming of the brother, and perhaps even more importantly from the point of view of her relationship with her brother, the growing up of the brother, seems highly relevant in another way. The main feeling about the brother seems to be fear. This comes out in many of the statements about him. He seems to have physically dominated her for many years. And this fear resulted in a particular form of defence, a stubborn silent resistance. From outside, this was, it seems, often interpreted as arrogance, overconfidence, an attempt to dominate. Here, certainly, is part of the 'problem with men'.

If we now look at the whole situation, we can see that it never changed or righted itself, so Peta could never forgive or re-evaluate it. The offence against her is still there, repeated every day. Neither her mother nor her brother would reconsider it, because they have not suffered in any way through it.

These are the areas which I would want to probe in working with this client. These are the hypotheses which I would want to check.

From a transpersonal point of view, there is something more to say. It seems to me that that my response to Peta fits very much into the framework suggested by Feinstein and Krippner (1988). She has a myth, that is a story which explains why she is the way she is. (This is the tale of the brother, his coming, the impossibility of her world at that point.) She has a countermyth, that is a story of what she did to contain it or compensate for it. (This the retreat into privacy, the refusal to identify, the need for safety and reassurance, the putting on of a mask which would get her by.) And what we could perhaps work together to discover is an integrating myth, that is something which goes beyond the categories and limits of the existing set-up. As Feinstein and Krippner (1988: 150) say: 'a new myth that resolves your original conflict'. We would look for helpful symbols in her dreams and fantasies, rather than trying to do the work entirely at the level of prose consciousness. This could in fact be an important part of the work.

It would not be essential: it is important not to have a programme which the client is expected to carry out. Because the human being is a system, we can intervene at any point and arrive at the same result in the end. But this mythological approach might appeal to someone who has spent so much time with books and fantasies.

Therapeutic possibilities

There is a real question here as to what the problem is. The original statement is, of course, 'A feminist's problem with men'. But as with many 'presenting problems', it changes a bit on closer examination. In the first place, there is just as much of a problem with authority figures as such – male or female – as there is with men. This comes out very clearly in the original statement, in fact. And, second, the problem with men seems questionable in the light of such statements by Peta as: 'It isn't exactly a problem with men. Maybe it's a *historical* problem with men, that's probably the case'. She goes on to say: 'At the moment I have a woman lover – which is rather happy and nice. She's a very interesting woman, and I'm hoping that whatever the form or shape of our relationship takes, I sure as hell need a good woman friend'.

So I think it would be a mistake to take the 'problem with men' as a primary concern. What seems more at issue is Peta's whole way of being in the world. My own approach is always to start with the area of maximum perceived pain: 'Where does it hurt most?' is the often unspoken question. From the answers which have been given, it seems to me that her relationships with her parents, and her brother, are quite central. So I would start from there.

It seems to me that straightforward regressive work would be all that would be needed to uncover the relevant repressed material. The only problem would be the resistance which would undoubtedly be present, and which could be expected to get in the way. This I would tackle in three ways: first, by building up rapport and trust; second, by working directly with the resistance; and third, by working indirectly.

In the first of these tasks, I would be helped by her affection for her father, which with any luck would be transferred in part on to me. I would be the good father, so to speak, that she never had but very much wanted – communicative and understanding. I would have to make sure that this did not become exaggerated into an idealization that could easily tip over into its opposite. This I could do by pointing out at any relevant point what was going on.

However, I would have to look out for any possibilities of my reproducing the behaviour of the father in a negative way. The most likely scenario here is that I would somehow remind her of her father's 'moral laziness' and his failures in 'empathetic generosity'. Any forgetfulness, any cavalier treatment, any forgetting of appointments or other arrangements, any failure to notify holidays well in advance, things like this could trigger off a powerful reaction which both of us could find hard to handle.

In the second of these tasks, I would be helped by excellent techniques I have developed over the years for working with resistance directly. This is done by the process of personification. Many times, when a person has said that she seems to have a block against doing something, I have asked her to draw a picture of the block, or put the block on a cushion and talk to it, or to speak for the block. This often results in a strong and effective piece of work, where the block is perhaps a parental voice, or some other important subpersonality or deeper potential.

In the third task, I would be helped by the transpersonal perspective I have already mentioned. By looking at symbols and metaphors (Grove and Panzer 1989) rather than actual memories of traumatic events, we can avoid the problems associated with the direct facing of pain. By working with metaphors instead of memories, we can avoid the ever-present danger of re-traumatizing the client. We can also avoid the dangers of false memory syndrome, that iatrogenic disease which seems to be spreading like wildfire in the USA, and is not unknown in this country.

It would be important not to be too single-minded about any one approach, but to deal with the material which Peta thought was important, whether or not it had to do with the key area I have outlined. This is Peta's work, not mine. However, it would probably be possible to get into the relevant area, since it is so similar to the area of maximum perceived pain. One would only have to encourage Peta to go further back with the same feelings as she is already experiencing. If the pain became too great to handle, more indirect methods could be used.

The course of therapy

My approach (primal integration) lays the major emphasis upon early trauma as the basic cause of mental distress, and enables people to regress back to the point in time where the trouble began, and to relive it there. This often involves a cathartic experience called 'a primal'. (Some people using this approach do not like this language, and instead call what they do regression-integration, or reintegration, or holonomic integration, or intensive feeling therapy.) It is strongly influenced by the work of Stanislav Grof (1975), who pointed to the deep traumas often associated with the experience of birth.

This is a syncretic approach, which brings together the extremes of therapy: it goes far back into what Wilber (1983) calls the pre-personal realm and deeply into the internal conflicts of the individual; and it goes far into the transpersonal realms of symbols, intuition and the deeper self (Rowan 1993). It is this combination of extremes which makes it so flexible in practice.

One of my main beliefs is that the person starts early. Memory can go back before language is acquired. People can often remember their own births. The foetus is conscious. All these statements are checkable, and in recent years more evidence has been appearing about them. Much of this material is now written up in Verny (1982), an excellent Canadian therapist. The full story about consciousness at birth is given by Chamberlain (1984, 1988).

This means that Swartley (1977) can write about eight major categories of trauma which may occur and be important in later life, all located in time between conception and the end of the first hour of life. Of these, the birth, uterine and implantation traumas are the ones which come up most frequently in therapy, though many practitioners in this field believe that conception trauma may come up more often if we allow it do so.

What this amounts to is an image of the person as essentially a healthy consciousness which may become visible as an ego at any point between conception and about three years old. Trauma can bring an ego into being very suddenly, as for example when there are definite memories of attempts at one's own abortion.

The person, now considered as definitely having an ego of some kind, has certain basic needs. When such primal needs are unmet by parents or other caregivers, or seem to be from the infant's point of view, the child will experience primal pain. And needs do not go away – they still remain – so the child has primal pain and unmet needs, too. This is what is meant by trauma.

This primal pain can be too much to bear. Lake (1980) describes four levels of experience. Level 1 is totally need-satisfying, everything is all right. Level 2 is coping: there are some unmet needs but they are bearable, still within the realm of the 'good enough'. Level 3 is opposition: pain of this order cannot remain connected up within the organism; it is repressed, and many aspects of the matter are pushed into the unconscious, in the manner suggested by Freud. Defences are then set up to preserve this solution, and to make sure that it stays forgotten. Level 4 is transmarginal stress (this term is taken from Pavlov's work) and here the pain is so great that the much more drastic defence of splitting has to be used. The whole self is split into two, and only one part (the 'false self' as described by Winnicott, 1958, and others) is adapted to the new situation, while the other part (Winnicott's 'true self') is hidden away as too small, too weak and too vulnerable. The self is then defined as not-OK or bad (this is now the false self, which is all that is present in awareness) and can even turn against itself, willing its own death and destruction. In this area, Reich, Balint, Winnicott, Janov, Grof and Laing are in substantial agreement, emphasizing that Level 4 is not an unusual response. The earlier the trauma, the fewer resources the infant has for dealing with it, and the more likely it is that the more drastic defence will be used. In this context, health is staying with the true self (real self) and disturbance is whatever leads to the setting up of a false self (unreal self). So in adult life, many people – not just a few – cultivate their false selves (persona, self-image, role, mask) rather than keeping or retaining touch with their true selves.

In considering trauma, it is important to realize that we are not necessarily talking about a single drastic event of some kind. The most common causes of neurosis are simply the common experiences of childhood – all the ways in which our child needs are unmet or frustrated. Hoffman (1979) has spoken eloquently about the problem of negative love. Because of the prevalence of neurosis and psychosis, vast numbers of parents are unable to give love to their children.

> When one adopts the negative traits, moods or admonitions (silent or overt) of either or both parents, one relates to them in negative love. It is illogical logic, nonsensical sense and insane sanity, yet the pursuit of the love they never received in childhood is the reason people persist in behaving in these destructive patterns. 'See, Mom and Dad, if I am just like you, will you love me?' is the ongoing subliminal query.
>
> (Hoffman 1979: 20)

As I say, this is not necessarily a single trauma, in the sense of a one-off event – that is much too simplistic a view. Rather, we would say with Balint (1968) that the trauma may come from a situation of some duration, where the same painful lack of 'fit' between needs and supplies is continued.

So if I adopt this approach, what am I really aiming at? The goal of primal integration is very simple and straightforward, and can be stated in one sentence. It is to contact and release the real self. Once that has been done, enormously useful work can be done in enabling the person to work through the implications of that, and to support the person through any life-changes that may result. But until the real self has been contacted, the process of working to release it will continue (see Rowan 1983: ch. 5). This is actually a very common notion in the whole field of psychotherapy, and by no means peculiar to this approach.

So primal integration keeps on coming back to the central value of reality, truth, authenticity, whatever you may like to call it – the main existentialist concern. Friedenberg (1973: 94) sums up this position thus:

> The purpose of therapeutic intervention is to support and re-establish a sense of self and personal authenticity. Not a mastery of the objective environment; not effective functioning within social institutions; not freedom from the suffering caused by anxiety – though any or all of these may be concomitant outcomes of successful therapy – but personal awareness, depth of real feeling, and, above all, the conviction that one can use one's full powers, that one has the courage to be and use all one's essence in the praxis of being.

My own position is to agree completely with this statement.

There would be no need to adopt any special or unusual methods with Peta. I would simply go ahead in my normal manner, which has been described more fully elsewhere (Rowan 1988). I think this would be highly suitable in the present case – in fact, it might have been tailor-made for a person like this, who desperately needs to recover her lost history.

Problem areas

Peta appears to have quite an active relationship with her mother, and this might raise difficulties when she digs up negative memories of her. There would be a temptation to confront her mother which the new data just uncovered. I would actively attempt to dissuade her from doing any such thing until the negative feelings had been well worked through in the therapeutic setting. I would explain that the therapy room is like an alchemical retort where various complex reactions are going on (McCurdy 1985). Unless it is sealed, there is every possibility of contamination from outside. It is better to let nothing in or out until the process is completed. Then the new and qualitatively different substance which emerges can engage in new and different ways with the world outside. In this case, a new Peta.

Similarly with the brother. She is unlikely to discover anything new about him, but even there she might. If he appears so dominant to her now, there must have been a time when he switched over from being smaller and weaker than Peta to being bigger and stronger than her. And this may have given rise to events of an aggressive nature, some of which may have been forgotten. If so, again I would attempt to dissuade her from confronting her brother about such things until the material had been better digested and processed. I am against provoking ugly incidents when they really refer to undigested material which is still being worked on.

And as already mentioned, there is the problem of pain. Is the pain of Peta's early traumas so great that she will avoid it at all costs?

> To force the client to recover these 'lost' memories can be harm-
> ful. Whatever protective mechanism has functioned for this
> client, she is now no longer able to recall in detail what hap-
> pened. She may not have the strength to face the events which
> happened at that time. Therefore, we work solely with what the
> client freely gives us.
>
> (Grove and Panzer 1989: 164)

It has been argued that all trauma is at bottom the fear of non-being, and for most of us this is the ultimate terror. The person may well feel that this is something which cannot be faced directly.

The use of symbol and metaphor is very useful in such a case. If the early events present themselves in such a form as 'It is like a black ball in my stomach', then I work with the black ball. If it is a smell, or 'I get this strange feeling around my solar plexus, like a square box', then I work with the square box. That is what I am given and that is what I can work with. In Peta's case, I would proceed very slowly and carefully, so as not to broach too suddenly a well of terror. But ultimately it may be this well of terror which has to be dealt with in some way or other.

A final difficulty might be with the question of her father. As already mentioned above, it would be important to avoid any sort of behaviour that might remind her of his failings. It would be important to keep a careful eye on the boundaries of our relationship, and the intactness of the therapeutic framework, so as not to be too close (suggesting threat) or too distant (suggesting abandonment).

Criteria for successful outcome

I would expect a good outcome in this instance, but it might well take some time to get there, given the strength of the screen memories and the presumed, therefore, strength of repression of the earlier trauma.

The process might be made more difficult by the fact that Peta has had training as a counsellor, and therefore might have more subtle and complex defences than the ordinary person. But in my experience this may delay matters, but does not sabotage them altogether. What we are talking about here, therefore, is a process taking at least two years, and probably more.

The desired outcome is the opening up and contacting of the real self by the client. There is, of course, always a danger in having a goal of any kind:

> If I acted out of my desire to heal the patient, I was setting myself up as the miracle worker. I would be doing it for my own satisfaction, for the joy of success, and maybe for the approval of my training analyst. My own needs would be in the foreground then, and the patient's needs would revert to the secondary position.
>
> (Singer 1972: 25)

So when I say that the desired outcome is that the client discover her real self, there is a danger that it is my goal and not hers. Yet in my heart of hearts I know that I could never be satisfied with half measures, such as enabling Peta to get on with authority figures enough to get by, or assisting her to get on better terms with men. All that would be good, but it would not be enough. Unless she is in touch with her real self, she cannot make the authentic choices which are what, I believe, she really wants and needs. This would then put her in the position, for example, of knowing for sure that her choice of a female lover was genuine and not phoney, open and not defensive, chosen and not compulsive.

Already we have some information to suggest that her relationship with her brother is improving: 'I met him briefly at mum's place, and he cried a bit, and he was angry, and I was able to say "Yes". And he looked at me with such astonishment . . . it was a nice moment'. We must not make too much of this, because he was in a vulnerable phase, and we do not know how she could cope with him in his strong phase. So here again I would say that she cannot really know how to treat her brother (or authority figures, or other men) until she has made contact with her real self.

And, finally, her relationship with her son. It must have been hard for Peta to know how to treat her son. On the one hand, she perhaps did not want to get too close to him, because this would repeat the pattern of her mother with her brother; on the other, she wouldn't want to deprive him, because this is what happened to her. Quite a tightrope to walk, especially if there is a strong fear of getting it wrong in case of terrible consequences. It may be too late to do anything much about all this, but at least a better awareness of what has happened must help her present relationship with him.

Summary

This has been an enormously interesting and satisfying piece of work for me. I have really enjoyed making contact with Peta, and wish I could work with her for real. If she, too, felt like that, I would feel privileged as a male therapist that she should trust me enough to open up in the way she already has. And as a man, I think it could be particularly fruitful to work through her feelings about men with me. There could be a real sense of working through her father stuff and coming out on the other side. Similarly in relation to the brother, I could see that working out well, too.

Of course, there is the mother stuff as well, and this might well turn out to be more important in the end. So often with women clients, I find that the father material is what comes up first, but that the material to do with the mother is in fact more fundamental. She might be able to work through that with me, or it might be that there could be a second or third phase of the therapy, which could be worked through more effectively with a female therapist. I am very much of the opinion that a single therapist can very seldom do all the work, and that male and female therapists do make a difference to what comes up and how it is handled.

Further reading

Balint, M. (1968). *The Basic Fault.* London: Tavistock.
Chamberlain, D.B. (1984). *Consciousness at Birth: A Review of the Empirical Evidence.* San Diego, CA: Chamberlain Communications.
Chamberlain, D.B. (1988). *Babies Remember Birth.* New York: Ballantine.
Dinnerstein, D. (1987). *The Rocking of the Cradle and the Ruling of the World.* London: Souvenir.
Eichenbaum, L. and Orbach, S. (1984). *What Do Women Want?* London: Fontana.
Feinstein, D. and Krippner, S. (1988). *Personal Mythology.* Los Angeles, CA: Tarcher.
Friedenberg, E.Z. (1973). *Laing.* London: Fontana/Collins.
Grof, S. (1975). *Realms of the Human Unconscious.* New York: Viking Press.
Grove, D.J. and Panzer, B.I. (1989). *Resolving Traumatic Memories.* New York: Irvington.
Hoffman, B. (1979). *No One is to Blame.* Palo Alto, CA: Science and Behaviour.
Lake, F. (1980). *Constricted Confusion.* Oxford: Clinical Theology Association.
McCurdy, A. (1985). Establishing and maintaining the analytical structure. In M. Stein (Ed.), *Jungian Analysis.* Boston, MA: Shambhala.
Rowan, J. (1976). *Ordinary Ecstasy.* London: Routledge and Kegan Paul.
Rowan, J. (1983). *The Reality Game.* London: Routledge and Kegan Paul.
Rowan, J. (1987). *The Horned God: Feminism and Men as Wounding and Healing.* London: Routledge.
Rowan, J. (1988). Primal integration. In J. Rowan and W. Dryden (Eds), *Innovative Therapy in Britain.* Milton Keynes: Open University Press.
Rowan, J. (1990). *Subpersonalities.* London: Routledge.
Rowan, J. (1993). *The Transpersonal in Psychotherapy and Counselling.* London: Routledge.
Singer, J. (1972). *Boundaries of the Soul.* New York: Anchor.
Swartley, W. (1977). Interviewed by John Rowan. *Self and Society,* Vol. 5/6, pp. 167–73.
Verny, T. (1982). *The Secret Life of the Unborn Child.* London: Sphere.
Wilber, K. (1983). *Eye to Eye.* Garden City: Anchor.
Winnicott, D. (1958). *Collected Papers.* London: Tavistock.

8

MAYE TAYLOR

FEMINIST PSYCHOTHERAPY

The therapist

I am a feminist and a counselling psychologist, with a special inter-est, training and many years of practice in feminist psychodynamic psychotherapy. In addition, I have a part-time post in a university where I teach, in particular an MSc in counselling psychology with an emphasis on feminist approaches. I also supervise research in related areas. I have a personal research and practice interest in the 'victim to patient process' in survivors of childhood sexual abuse and using the post-traumatic stress disorder model to aid under-standing and treatment. For many years, I have acted as consultant to various organizations in the area of equal opportunity training programmes.

For me, feminism is a process that starts with recognizing the inferior status of women, moves on to an analysis of the specific forms and causes of that inequality, and involves identifying and recommending strategies of change. These include recognizing and validating women's realities, women's interpretations and women's unique contributions. The aim must be equality of condition and not just equality of opportunity. Feminist therapy is one such strat-egy, but is in no way an alternative to political action. Both are needed. One extra note here: I acknowledge that there are many 'feminisms'. The definition I give here is a working definition which I have found a useful model for therapy.

Jean Baker Miller (1978) described power as 'the capacity to pro-duce change', and if psychotherapy is about anything it is also about producing change. Feminist therapy carries the extra dimension of recognizing that for women, at least, transforming their lives is not simply a matter of their individual strengths and efforts, for the values and mental health of women are so inextricably intertwined with the social structures. It is not all that long ago, in the order of things, when men ran the lives of women and children on a dominance–submission model. Only men could vote, own property or sign contracts. In legal discourse, women were excluded from personhood. A wife was the chattel of her husband. He had the legal right to enforce this with physical chastisement. Whereas a man's labour was located in the public sphere of production and valued, women's labour was seen to belong to the apolitical private sphere and marginal. The suffrage movement – comprising women of enormous courage – did win women the right to vote in 1920, but they could only vote for men! Subsequently, the task of feminists has been to challenge the depoliticization of the 'personal' and to highlight the social nature of sexuality, birth control, domestic labour and child-rearing in particular.

As a feminist psychotherapist, I see my role as helping women to identify choices in their lives; to regain power and control which many of them lost as children and who have had their 'personhood' denied both systematically and interpersonally; and to live their lives as they see fit, rather than as 'significant others' may wish them to do. Central to this is helping women to begin to see and believe there are alternatives and possibilities for their lives that they hitherto have been unable to see. The starting point of psychodynamic theory is not society but the individual. I see its task as enabling the person to close the gap between her illusory and actual fulfilment of her needs – the important 'making conscious' process. For feminists this is only the beginning and recognizes that social change is needed as well as individual change. Further, there is the stark constrast of feminist psychotherapists with many mainstream psychiatrists for example, who are so impressed with their advancement of knowledge of the chemistry of the nervous system and the improvement of some depressed persons with medication, that they consider depression to be an inherited physiological condition to be treated primarily by medication. Intra- and interpersonal change is not necessary or even relevant. We know from the mental health statistics that large numbers of women are treated for depression solely by drugs. This is enormously disempowering to the woman. It is informing her that only medication, not her own insights and changes, can benefit her. It is also denying the lived realities of women's lives. The goals of feminist psychodynamic therapy are to enable the woman to understand the multiplicity of influences that motivate her feelings, thoughts and actions, so that she can experience more control and exercise more direction in her own life.

Further information requested

The further questions I asked are reproduced below. I have summarized Peta's answers, highlighting the issues which seemed to me to be significant for therapy.

You say you've got a problem with men. Could you tell me how you know this? What is the evidence you use?
Peta's answer opened with a very firm 'I do feel I've got a problem with some men in authority', but then she qualifies this by saying 'No it's all figures in authority', and then 'No, it's actually against guys and blokes and male persons because your dad was not there'. She acknowledged that the very process of thinking about my question had moved her on a little, but that she was still left being aware of the *reality* of sexism, and that this troubled her not only in her personal life but in her counselling work. She described sexism as often being very subtle, like racism, and how this presented difficulties for her in identifying why she was sometimes hurt by 'chance comments'. Peta also volunteered that she has read *Women in Therapy and Counselling* three times as evidence of what she is trying to work on.

You mention your reaction to your partner's withdrawal as seeing him as using silence as a weapon. Could you tell me more about how it makes you feel, and what you do in response?
Peta recollects being *so* angry when she looks back on the relationship with Tom in France; she describes trembling from head to foot and being in a state of shock. She elaborates on this by describing it as 'a state of being in which one is absolutely consumed with rage, one is completely taken over'. She adds that she experienced the same state when watching a film as part of her counselling course. The film was, in her words, by two eminent researchers doing things on maternal deprivation and despair and withdrawal. She reveals that she has been able to connect the two events, and that it has meant that she has discovered it is OK when she gets angry when something really important happens. She now feels that this is a major breakthrough, and that joyfulness and tranquility are more available to her because of having those experiences. She does qualify this by adding that the 'explosion' in France was awful because she couldn't actually talk to anyone for the two weeks; but she was proud of the way she was able to protect herself and used her own inner resources. Knowing more about silences means that she can now recognize hostile silences and is thus more alert to it. She does not just experience it as a brick wall, which it might be; but

then she can ask what's behind the brick wall? Peta added that she does not particularly do anything about it, but just understands it.

I liked your phrase 'grass-hopping'. Please do some more . . . just tell me some more things about your memories that you consider significant of your mother, father and brother.
Peta indicated that she liked the question, acknowledging that I had mentioned three people who represent her nuclear family, that is 'the sort of closest to me biologically', but then adds that as she 'grows hopefully into an outrageous middle age that biology does not have the same meaning as it did when I was younger'. She indicates some sadness in her reflection that women have too much power over kids and men have a different kind of power as fathers which they don't understand. She talks about the frighteningly vulnerable dependency a child has and how she is so much more aware of this; how she is aware that by being a single parent she is in some way replicating something that was not good for her, being brought up really by her mother. Peta is proud of what she has managed to achieve single-handedly, but is constantly monitoring her own parenting . . . and very aware of the power she has over her child. She likes the way that she is able to be herself at home, knowing at times that she is 'impossible', but being able to acknowledge that it 'won't rip the innards out of the whole thing', because she is able to talk and share her awareness of what she is doing with her son.

You speak of it being easy for you to feel close to Hamish in a 'therapeutic sense'. What is the difference for you between this and 'ordinary' closeness with men?
'I feel very close to Hamish, I actually like Hamish very much', and she adds that she is 'plotting the way I experience how much I enjoy Hamish's company', and compares it with good supervision in that you throw things out and rapidly get something back.

I notice you link fear of mother and wanting coalitions and equality. Please could you tell me more about this.
Peta's answer is short and whispered. She indicates that the desperately wanted better communication with her mother, while at the same time acknowledging what her mother did give her. Yet there were huge tensions between them, particularly during adolescence, when Peta describes how she would have liked to just walk out. She finishes with, 'it comes forcibly, when I needed it most there were no coalitions: she wasn't there and neither was my father'.

*You refer to your conditioning as a woman, and not wanting to compete
as a result. I would like you to tell me a little more about how you
experienced this conditioning.*
Peta's response was 'I find that a large question'. She said she could
answer in contemporary terms in that she finds she is vastly over-
sensitive to situations where she might voice her considered professional views. If a man is dismissive in any way, she is prone to over-
react. She goes on to comment about how for many years she was
completely disconnected from school, how she was very bored and
dissociated and how that led her to fail the eleven-plus. She laughed
when remembering that she was believed to be backward at that
stage, and put in the lowest stream of the secondary modern school!
In actuality, she was contemptuous of what the school had to offer;
Peta says she saw no reason to compete, was not doing very much,
and still won't compete now, which she thinks makes her unemploy-
able. She is currently on income support and doesn't *have* to work,
which she likes. However, Peta says that this has its costs. She wishes
people to take her more seriously and yet knows this has been a life-
long problem for her, a difficulty in seeing that she should make
other people take her seriously. She acknowledges that she sells
herself short.

*Your response to people saying 'it doesn't matter whether you are a man
or a woman' is that it is 'displacing'. I am intrigued . . . what do you
mean?*
Peta acknowledges that as she speaks about this, that the veins of
rage in her could so easily be tapped into; that her relationship to
whether she is a man or a woman is underpinned by seams of rage
that have not yet found expression; and that she feels she has to be
very careful with those feelings less they atomize the entire cosmos.
She feels very strongly that it *does* matter that she is a woman and
not a man, because in actuality that gets rammed down her throat.
There is no getting away from it. The black consciousness movement of the 1960s was very important in forming her political
awareness of difference, and gives her the responsibility of speaking
out. She feels she has a moral obligation to sisterhood.

*I would like to know a little more about how you felt in your gay rela-
tionships and something about your expectations of those relationships as
against your heterosexual ones . . . if you could find something to say.*
Peta was quick to point out that she had really only had one gay
relationship, and that it had been a long time ago and that it did
not last very long. But she felt quite blessed by it, and it had 'blasted
everything into bits and things settled down into interesting new

shapes afterwards'. She indicated that she had learnt a lot from it about the quality of human relationships and the passion involved, not needing to be tied to status or description of the person. She mentions feeling very passionate about her mother. It also made her ponder on whether women are impelled to develop same-sex relationships because of the nature of things. She went on to mention psychological background and the need to read about the Oedipus complex according to Chodorow!

Anything more you want to say to me now after my questions?
'Well it gives me quite a warm feeling, I suppose at the most primitive level it's having serious attention paid to one'. Peta went on to say that she did not want that to sound flippant, that she minded very much and that she was glad to have the opportunity to talk to somebody who 'let the whole person be involved in counselling'. She explained that she does not respond very well to a detached person. She remembers with some anger going to a counsellor when she was really very unhappy and incapacitated by depression after she was divorced. She was also very angry and swore a lot, and the counsellor said, 'I really would prefer if you don't use that language'. Peta never went back. As she said, when a person is struggling for meaning you can so easily cut the ground from under their feet.

Assessment

I am not comfortable with the power dimension of the word 'assessment', but will take it on board to mean looking at suitability for feminist psychodynamic psychotherapy. Such an assessment would ordinarily involve Peta making her own assessment as to whether she would feel comfortable working with me, as much as my looking for signs that Peta could benefit from the sort of work I do, exploring the possibility that we could form a therapeutic alliance as well as be able to work in the transference. It is a momentous thing to do, to choose to take somebody into therapy. You are involving the person in an adventure, taking them on a guided tour of their own experience in a relationship which is quite different from any other; and this carries awesome responsibility, as well as supreme privilege. The process and outcomes are vital to the person who seeks therapy. So, given the initial information, and her response to my questions, yes please, I will work with Peta. I have a very warm positive reaction to her – too early to call it counter-transference, but clear enough to suggest that the dynamic between us would be a creative and exciting one, making the working alliance challenging as well as supportive. In addition, she satisfies two important criteria for my approach, for not only is she psychologically minded but she is a declared feminist and demonstrates social and political awareness. The major issues that she presents, including problems with men, damaged self-concept, fear of rejection, coping with her anger, concerns about how she parents her son, dealing with power (her own and others) and the implications of all of these 'concerns' for her decision to become a counsellor, will best suit feminist therapy.

First, to discuss my judgement that Peta's needs would be better met within a feminist therapy approach. Traditional psychotherapy tends to focus primarily, if not exclusively, on internal or intrapsychic conflicts rather than on the cultural context that has produced them. This emphasis serves to divert energy from an awareness of the social and political context, and the need for change. It also fosters in women a sense of uniqueness regarding their 'pathology'. Feminist psychodynamic psychotherapy does not maintain a narrow, single-minded focus on either intrapsychic or sociocultural realities. Peta, both in her own comments and in her answers to my questions, demonstrates that she has already gone a long way to understanding that much of her current concerns and distress stem from patriarchal society's neglect and distortion of women's (and thus her) true intellectual, sexual and social needs. While acknowledging the uniqueness of her 'symptoms', I assume it is legitimate to view the social and cultural context of her problems as an important focus in therapy. Peta's capacity to identify and respond to the ways in which women generally are depreciated, trivialized, scapegoated or falsely defined in work and family, and thus be able to work on a process of *self*-definition and growth, will be crucial. This will involve rejecting any notion of self as conceived outside culture and gender relations. She is clearly not naive in seeing this as simply a matter of 'making choices', but can see the restrictions of her personal history, the distancing of her father, *and* the relative power of men.

Peta has clearly had to, and still does, battle with culturally defined notions of masculinity and femininity, and how consciously or unconsciously these concepts reflect what is seen as healthy or 'natural' for her and all women and men. She says she has problems with men, that she has problems with her anger affecting her relationships with men and she does not want to be so angry with them: she sees her feminism as perhaps problematic, commenting about how she feels self-conscious that 'I must tell you that I am a feminist'. I was very drawn to this. It will be important to work with Peta in the transference relationship with those feelings, using the process of 'conscious partiality' which will enable us to separate out those things which are uniquely hers and those things which we share by virtue of our common gender. Peta talks about how she can do the sociopolitical analysis very well but wants to get away from the consequences of patriarchy, of 'being turned away' from.

Let us now turn to my other criterion, 'psychological-mindedness', which has several ingredients. While reading what Peta had said, I held several questions in my head:

1 Has she the capacity to recognize and tolerate her internal reality, with its wishes and conflicts, and distinguish this from her external reality? Clearly, this is the case with Peta. Several times she acknowledges inner material – she talks about her 'projected anger'; for example, which is a strong indicator. As I have already discussed, she does describe her external reality well: 'As a female single parent' is just one phrase out of many.

2 I think, too, that Peta does enjoy introspection. In her initial account, she reveals that she has done a lot already in her musing about her childhood and the influences on her current state. Her responses to my questions reveal that she has enjoyed the process of being asked to do just that. She has a lively curiosity and a real concern about her own internal reality, which will be vital. Her kind of drive and interest in the sources of psychic pain in herself will be the greatest possible help in therapy: it sustains the alliance.

3 The last point links in well with another of my queries: Does Peta have the capacity to see the relationship between different sections of her history and her present discomforts? Clearly she does. She herself talks about seeing her life as a series of crises, and identifies some of the crucial ones, such as the death of her father, her marriage, the birth of her son and her divorce. She also links her experiences at primary school, for example, with her reluctance to compete now, and she can see the costs of this.

4 I looked for the amount of distance there was from Peta's emotional experience. There is no evidence of any severe denial, repression or indeed splitting as a way of coping. Quite the contrary, Peta shows a readiness to handle her emotional experience. The way she herself distinguishes her response to her partner's use of silence, for example, demonstrates this. Her 'affects' in her responses appear entirely appropriate too. She brings forward different memories with different qualities. Her delightful phrase 'grass-hopping' is a good pointer to the fact that she was monitoring her own performance and noticing her feelings.

5 I was also looking for the capacity to free-associate, or at least signs that it could develop, that is did Peta show that she was

reflecting on herself in a new way as a result of being listened to? This evidence was there. Peta did elaborate and extend her train of thought several times, as evidenced by her 'thinking out loud' about her relationship with her mother and her regrets there. This reassures me that there is little severe inhibition or chronic anxiety. Certainly, I did not get the impression that there was extreme passive dependency. Quite the reverse!

6 One of the truisms often used by therapists, is the 's/he who fails at everything will fail at therapy'. Perhaps this is a bit over-deterministic, but given the enormity of the therapeutic enterprise it is helpful at least to consider. Evidence of some success in any area, be it study, work or an important relationship with an accompanying degree of self-esteem can form a solid basis for some self-respect in the working alliance. Peta says she is proud of the job she has done as a single parent and obviously gets pleasure from that as well as other parts of her life.

7 The capacity to use the imagination is also strongly linked in psychotherapy research with good outcomes; the use of metaphor being a crucial part of the therapeutic discourse. Peta, with her background in art therapy, 'has the right credentials' . . . but not just that; in her own story she displays a vivid imagination and use of metaphor – that grasshopper again.

Assessment is necessarily speculative, but given my observations about Peta's capacity to work psychologically and sociologically, my considered view is that my approach would help her resolve the issues that she herself identifies. It is important that she has already done a lot of the preparatory work. She comes to therapy with an agenda, and with a clear view of what she wants; and equally important, what she does *not* want.

Therapeutic possibilities

I start with Peta's own words: 'I have a sense that the deep past does have a profound influence on what I'm walking round in, in the present'; and 'If I sense that a person is unable to look at gender issues, or there is tension around that, then I will withdraw'. Here, in just two of the many similar statements, lie the foundations of why I consider that feminist psychodynamic therapy offers Peta the best chance of resolution of her declared concerns and distress. A psychodynamic approach will allow me to work directly in the area where the effects of the phallocentric discourse are felt – the unconscious – enabling Peta to become fully conscious of the gap that exists between the illusory and the actual fulfilment of her needs.

This will include identifying and acknowledging that some of her distress can be seen as her resistance to oppression, which conversely has worked against her best interests at times. This is evidenced, for example, in her 'doing without a career', rather than risk rejection thus depriving her of an arena in which she could put her talents to good use, and perhaps have a stronger sense of her own self-worth. She is training in counselling but can see trouble ahead in that for herself.

Her relationship with her mother is one of the areas she identifies, so woman-to-woman therapy will offer Peta the possibility of looking to me, her therapist, for mirroring, and thus let her fantasize herself as omnipotent in 'selfish' ways. This is so important for Peta. It will enable her to step outside her current state of feeling responsible for everything – a state which she communicates in her comments, and about which she may well be not fully aware. Certainly she talks about men's reactions to her in ways which suggest that she feels it is up to her to change, that is, it looks as though at an unconscious level she *does* feel that she has to take responsibility for them too. Crucially, she will not need to be responsible for me. Therapy will give her a safe space within which to test out her developing new ways of being autonomous, feeling what it is like to have 'power' to change if that is what she wants, rather than it being required of her to get attention. Put another way, it should help her stop engaging in crude bouts of centre-staging to demonstrate a sense of power which is not there.

Another possibility is that she will be able to experience her strong feelings, and express them. She can rage at her therapist. Testing out me, her therapist, and my ability to survive her anger, will be a crucial part of the transference between us. It offers her the scope to experience very different outcomes to expressed strong feelings. There is an important gender difference here. This 'getting in touch with feelings' is not without dangers if feelings like rage and anger are involved. It is acceptable for women to express what is seen as appropriately female emotions such as tenderness. But the reality for many women is that family situations mean they have to suppress the expression of feelings to avoid provoking violent responses. Peta is aware of this in current situations, but it is important for Peta to separate out the influence of early relationships and later and current influences, not only on what she feels but how she expresses those feelings. Therapy with another woman will provide the possibility of really getting in touch with quite primitive feelings, without fear of rejection or reprisal. She does comment about being able to rage and storm at home, but I notice that this is tinged with some concern about the effect this has on her son. Therapy will offer the safe environment to explore just what it is she is feeling, and what happens when she lets herself feel and express those feelings without any thought for the effect it is having on another person.

The course of therapy

The course of this therapy will proceed like any other – meeting, exploring issues, making a contract, establishing the relationship, fostering insight, working on and through the issues with resolution in mind. Briefly, this means that Peta and I will be engaged in a process of psychological treatment in which we will attempt to bring about a change in Peta's beliefs and behaviour by assisting her to acquire increased insight into her emotional life. This will involve putting considerable emphasis on the development and maintenance of the working alliance by my identifying and enlisting Peta's intellectual and emotional assets. In addition, the wider context of the therapy is important here. Feminism challenges the androcentric way in which therapy has and is currently conceptualized and practised, as well as the way in which therapists are trained and supervised. Feminist therapy is not a set of techniques or conclusions. The specific techniques are less important than the philosophy behind their use. Above all, it aims to empower through the working alliance. Peta will not be 'reduced' to a collection of hormones, bodily parts and emotions. The feminist psychological conceptual shift from 'sex' to 'gender' has brought about a revolutionary change in assumptions about the causes of female behaviour and will underpin any 'explanations' that I use as a basis for interpretation.

My work with Peta will start by viewing her biological sex as forming the basis of the very influential social classification system, namely gender, which she has experienced. And, conceptualizing that, not as a property of Peta as an individual, but as a principle of all social organizations which have influenced her, there will thus be a significant emphasis on social factors as well as intrapsychic ones. Use will also be made of an adapted Maslow hierarchy in locating, organizing and confronting Peta's issues. I work with the assumption that a manifestation of distress and disturbance at any of the five levels may be the outcome of disturbance at other levels, and I will examine how they have combined and are combining in her current situation. The following is an outline of the adapted hierarchy:

- *Existential:* life choices Peta has already made.
- *Personality:* this concerns the 'psychopathology' which she herself sees as problematic. She often refers to unreasonable anger.

- *Interaction:* her close relationships and current loneliness. She expresses a desire for a more long-term sexual relationship.
- *Predicament:* her immediate situation. She is a single mother, which has very real consequences for the way she lives her life.
- *Material position:* money, housing, etc. In Peta's case, this is a very restricted income.

Facilitating Peta to clarify the relationship between these various factors, and thus make sense of responses which she currently finds puzzling and problematic, can be best achieved by elaborating all those counselling skills which are particularly feminist in their intent and focus, in the context of psychodynamic theory. Indeed, there is a sense in which women have engaged in a form of counselling for centuries. The skills of the 'wise woman healers' have always been in demand in communities. Peta herself has these skills; training in counselling is further equipping her. Indeed, two of the 'core conditions' of say humanistic counselling, 'empathy' and 'unconditional positive regard', can be seen in Western typifications of what is ideally feminine. For my purposes here, I take empathy to be about feelings in relationship to knowledge; in order to respond empathically to Peta, it is crucial for me to be able to experience her emotional world in the 'here and now', and also to understand the personal and social history of that world.

I am a woman therapist and a declared feminist, Peta is a woman client – this will form a substantive part of the therapeutic alliance. Given Peta's expressed disappointment and anger with the relationship she had with her mother, as well as the love she felt for her, it will be a vital part of therapy to acknowledge and address her unmet 'daughter needs' and to provide an experience of consistent caring that she can ingest in the present. Peta needs to have an intimate mother–daughter relationship in therapy, paradoxically so that she can actually separate from the real mother and build a stronger sense of her self. The rationale for this lies in the way that Peta expresses very strongly what she did not get from her mother. Her use of the word 'coalition' is important, for at its best that is what this therapy will give her.

Peta's active participation in negotiating the contract is sought. At this stage, I suggest once weekly therapy for a period of twelve months, allowing for the possibility that it be extended to twice weekly and/or two years if Peta finds it helpful. I will declare my expressed intention to avoid diagnostic labels and the use of technical terms that would serve to establish a dominant 'expert' model. I will state the intention, and strive to make the relationship between us an egalitarian one: this is not to deny the power relationship that

exists in therapy, but to say that this power imbalance will be acknowledged, considered and monitored, particularly with reference
to transference and counter-transference interpretations. I will most
certainly indicate my readiness to work therapeutically with Peta,
but not promise 'cure'. But I will use my professional skills and
knowledge for her benefit, explaining what those are so that she can
make her decision after meeting me and discussing how I work. In
effect, the course of therapy will involve playing close attention to

• the nature of the therapeutic relationship between us;
• the causes of her psychological distress;
• my interpretation of her problems and symptoms;
• her goals for therapy.

Given the restrictions of this particular enterprise, namely a chapter in a book, I end this section by extracting a major theme to
illustrate. Peta uses the word 'power' a number of times, as well as
describing situations that were 'about' power. Our therapeutic relationship will need to fully explore what she wanted from her mother
or father, but seemingly could not get; her very poignant comment
about how it did not help to be *told* that her father 'adored her',
when he never showed it, reveals the extent of the longing that she
has had to suppress. It will be important to work on differences, the
difference between 'power *to*', which will allow Peta freedom to
make choices rather than be 'compelled' by inner tensions; and to
free herself from needing to have 'power *over*' others as a way of
protecting her own rather fragile self. She appears to be, from her
self-descriptions, a rather difficult combination of vulnerability and
abrasiveness! Her need to subvert facilitators is a manifestation,
perhaps, of this confusion about power.

Problem areas

Feminist psychodynamic therapy is not easy. It is not a 'soft option'.
Criticisms that it is merely a cosy and collusive discussion of ideo-
logical points of agreement between feminists belie the exacting
requirements of working with both intrapsychic life and the social
structures. This can lead to two distinct types of problems: problems
within therapy and problems arising out of therapy, which might
threaten it and bring about premature termination.

Peta is a feminist, and sees herself as being aware of the political
nature of some of her distress. However, I suspect that her awareness
that 'the personal is political' will not prevent her being overwhelmed
when she gets in touch with exactly what that has meant for her.

I feel that Peta is perhaps not fully aware of the full extent of how achieving what she wants for herself might prove costly: backlash exists, and achieving her personal aims in therapy might just make some parts of her life more difficult. To explain: I think Peta, like many women, has a deep-rooted fear of destroying the love of those closest to her through her own aggression and denigrating attitudes. This is often insurmountable in women: losing the approval of others is more painful for them than being oppressed and could prove difficult for Peta too. What Peta has decided is that she wants to use her capabilities freely, to arrive at her own decisions independently, to struggle for a change in her own conduct and that of others, and to overcome her fear of inevitable aggression. Perhaps she is not completely aware that women who do possess power must reckon with loss of love. Sadly, such women are often destined to be hated, not only by men but also by other women who feel powerless by comparison. Could this be the 'Margaret Thatcher syndrome' Peta was thinking of?

Drawing on my 'conscious partiality' makes me very familiar with the rage that Peta and we all feel as working women, as partners, or as mothers, when we are expected to be responsible for anything and everything while lacking the power to change things. Or when women, out of fear of rejection, do not desire that power, and are full of envy for women who do. As women we are as inclined as ever to convert our underlying anger into self-reproach and self-sacrifice, and thus practise a form of passive aggression that is unsatisfactory to both ourselves and those whom it affects. Peta wants equality: she says she wants to shout 'give it to me'. Yes, women want to change the relations between the sexes, but they will never do so without anger and pain: conflicts are inevitable and they have to be worked through. Working through them is hard, making this fully conscious carries enormous pain, and the concomitant risk for Peta is finding that during therapy she is angrier than ever.

If Peta succeeds in making conscious the unconscious motives that lie at the root of her behaviour, she might well find that unconscious guilt feelings are there in abundance, so undoing the tenacious defence mechanisms that she erected. This will be very painful, given that she has worked very hard to separate from her past. It is possible that Peta could drop out of therapy if she became overwhelmed by those repressed guilt feelings, particularly as she has some expectations that she has 'sussed out' for herself much what is going on. It might prove too big a challenge to her self-image. Peta has herself identified that there might be problems here. She talked about subverting a tutor who was making psychodynamic interventions in personal territory that she found deeply, deeply threatening, and so she withdrew. A feminist psychodynamic perspective will produce similar threats and conflicts, particularly in Peta's understanding of herself and drawing parallels with her mother, and thus then understanding her mother in similar ways, creating considerable ambivalence. Blaming one's mother carries strong overtones of guilt for feminists, who draw attention to the wider cultural context in which mothering takes place. An 'idealized' mother transference relationship with me might be just too much to bear. It is at this point that Peta, like many women would revert back to her previous strategy of splitting that enables her to carry the disappointment of the early years. I might have to become the 'bad mother' and thus be rejected. Therapy could be very stormy and take considerably longer.

Having said all that, however, I am still of the opinion that the 'adventure' is worth pursuing.

Criteria for successful outcome

A major difference between traditional psychotherapeutic interventions and feminist approaches can be found in this whole area of 'desirable outcomes'. Traditionally, psychotherapy goals, which should become outcomes, are generally divided into three categories:

1 Remission of pathological symptoms and behaviours.
2 Ratings of the client's behaviours by others as 'normal'.
3 Evidence of interpersonal or community social competence, such as maintaining a household and holding down a job.

Although these goals to some degree might underpin feminist approaches, the emphasis is on empowerment, egalitarianism and change, both for one's self and for one's effective environment. Adjustment to oppressive environments or conditions is not a valued outcome. Consequently, in my work with Peta I did not carry into it a predetermined and specific set of goals. There are no carefully laid out criteria other than Peta's own agenda. I certainly have general aims of my approach in mind, but it must be Peta who decides whether the 'outcomes' satisfy her. Naturally, or I would not be using it, I believe that grounding psychodynamic therapy in a feminist perspective makes it a very powerful intervention in women's lives, that is in the type of concerns that Peta herself raises about the quality of her life now and in the future, particularly in terms of her relationships with men.

Having identified that sometimes she is afraid of men because of their power, a positive outcome of the therapy would be a reduction in that fear. She describes the pain she feels when men she respects turn away from her, and she interprets that turning away as being because they feel disempowered by her. The fact that her father was distant is influential. Her therapy could not change how men feel, or make her brother talk to her, but a positive outcome of therapy would be that she could reflect on what if anything she could do; what was her part, if any in it; and to identify and eliminate if she so wishes those aspects of her behaviour that are unnecessarily threatening. Grieving for what she never had with her father, and to stop looking for compensation for that deficit in her male relationships and to enjoy them in a more autonomous way, is certainly possible for her. Peta said she wanted to shout at men, 'give me equality'. Feminist therapy is a vehicle for experiencing oneself as equal, and offers the chance to carry those feelings out into other relationships. She would not need men to 'give her equality'.

It is my sense that there will be many positively indicated outcomes of therapy, in that Peta will be able to stop 'trying to cure her measles by rubbing out the spots'. The idea behind the adapted Maslow hierarchy is that by locating the source of her 'symptoms' (distress) more finely, she will confront them more successfully, one by one.

Finally, experiencing psychodynamic interpretations as helping foster insight and thus allowing her access to her own unconscious is to give her back control. I would like the interaction between us to be memorable in its own right, a truly human encounter with both our 'whole persons engaged'. I hope that she would experience our therapeutic relationship as a coalition, something she clearly desires. Outcomes need not just be in terms of changes in functioning, but also in terms of the validating experience of the therapeutic process.

Summary

I liked Peta from the outset. I wanted to work with her so that the difference between 'knowing' and 'knowing about', as a gap between intimacy and acquaintance, could be spanned. Like Christiane Olivier, I too reached the point in my work as a psychotherapist where I could no longer stand apart from my women clients and play dumb: the opaque mirror stance can be punitive. Like her, I cannot separate what I am from what I know. The things I 'heard' from Peta put me in touch with a world that I recognize as my own. Much of her history ('herstory') was mine. Identifying with her did not mean that essential boundaries could not be kept. Intimacy is not the same as fusion.

An end note: why do we have to have a *feminist* therapy? I find it very sad that the struggle for women's liberation has sometimes been so grossly distorted, for women are as much as ever the victims of limited opportunities for promotion, low wages, the double burden of home and career, subject to unprecedented levels of violence in the street and in the home . . . but the prevailing reaction to all of this is at best one of indifference or of poking fun at feminists. In many areas of the world the status of women continues to be not only reprehensible, as in ours, but a clear affront to human dignity. The consciousness of women is the consciousness of the subordinate. Such a climate allows one national newspaper to have the headline, 'Terrified husband has to lie by the side of wife whilst she is raped'.

Yes, we do need a feminist perspective in therapy.

Further reading

These are just a few books I have found particularly illuminative and helpful.

Benjamin, J. (1990). *The Bonds of Love*. London: Virago.
Burman, E. (Ed.) (1989). *Feminists on Psychological Practice*. London: Sage.
Chodorow, N. (1978). *The Reproduction of Mothering*. Berkeley, CA: University of California Press.
Faludi, S. (1992). *Backlash: The Undeclared War Against Women*. New York: Chatto and Windus.
Ford, J. and Sinclair, R. (1987). *Sixty Years On: Women Talk About Old Age*. London: Women's Press.
Gilligan, C. (1982). *In a Different Voice*. Cambridge, MA: Harvard University Press.
Jacobs, M. (1992). *Psychodynamic Counselling in Action*. London: Sage.
Johnson, M. (1988). *Strong Mothers – Weak Wives*. Berkeley, CA: University of California Press.
Miller, J. Baker (1978). *Towards a New Psychology of Women*. Harmondsworth: Penguin Books.
Olivier, C. (1989). *Jocasta's Children: The Imprint of the Mother*. London: Routledge.
Sayers, J. (1991). *Mothering Psychoanalysis*. London: Hamish Hamilton.
Showalter, E. (1987). *The Female Malady: Women, Madness and English Culture*. London: Virago.
Ussher, J. (1991). *Women's Madness: Mysogyny or Mental Illness?* Hemel Hempstead: Harvester Wheatsheaf.
Walker, M. (1990). *Women in Therapy and Counselling*. Milton Keynes: Open University Press.

9

CHRISTINE WOOD

ART THERAPY

The therapist

The process of therapy depends upon a relationship: essentially when a client is searching for a therapist, she is searching for someone with whom she can make a relationship. Of course, the focus is not the same as in other relationships; in therapy, the client's sense of the need for exploration and change is central. The therapist's task is to help the client become more aware of her own needs.

Sometimes it is said that there are as many schools of art therapy as there are art therapists. This is an exaggeration. However, when I think back to those ideas and ways of working which have influenced my practice, there are indeed a great many. It is hard for me to synthesize and describe the many strands which have helped me weave my own therapist's cloak and my own approach to the work.

I trained as an art therapist at Goldsmiths College in London, between 1977 and 1978. Memories of my training include the course leader's fierce social conscience, and equally fierce belief that it is possible to work therapeutically with most people – as her students we would be working with people with social and economic needs. Such ideas were rarely fashionable in psychotherapeutic circles and they have become even less so. In Community Health Sheffield, the art therapists try to ensure that they work with clients who are not normally offered the benefits of psychotherapy – those who have long-term mental health problems, perhaps a history of psychosis, elderly people, people with terminal illness, with learning difficulties or people hurt in accidents.

Other influences have been the writings of Winnicott on transitional space, and Bettelheim's stress on the significance of the environment. Students of art therapy with whom I have worked have helped me to retain a strong sense of the magic of art making within art therapy, while recent work with a shaman psychotherapist brought alive an interest in the ancient, time-served methods of healing through rituals, legends and the telling of stories. The London Women's Therapy Centre gave me much when I was based in London, particularly in its attempts to demystify the process of therapy. Training events run by the Institute of Group Analysis and the Tavistock Institute have sometimes been gruelling but have helped me test myself, and develop a real belief that I know how to swim in choppy therapeutic waters. In the NHS, I have been fortunate to work for long periods with two very compassionate psychiatrists, Alec Jenner and Jim Gomersall, who both encourage staff to develop their own style of work. Both believe strongly in acknowledging the power and the responsibility of the client. My supervisor, Lily Barker, originally a social worker and now employed by MIND, has for many years been a source of strength and courage.

The people who have taught me most about this strange trade have been the people who have been 'patient' enough to be my clients. I continue to be amazed at how generously people share their thoughts, feelings, images and lives, contributing our understanding of the relationship between internal and external experience. A great deal more could still be done to help people to recognize their own contribution to what happens in their therapy.

Further information requested

I have been living with Peta's words from her original conversation with Moira Walker. Reading what someone has to say about herself is very different from meeting with her and hearing what she has to say.

I cannot see her (although I have made different pictures of her in my head, drawn from Moira's thumb-nail sketch). I do not know how she is sitting or what her face is doing. I cannot hear inflections or different tones in her voice, which might mean that I put a very different emphasis on what she describes. All this makes a difference to my understanding of the form her feelings take. For Peta, too, I imagine being unable to see the therapists whom she is addressing is a little bizarre.

When I first read what Peta says of herself, I had a sense of her skating over the surface of what she feels. Re-reading it I realize there is a great deal there about feeling. What seems central, now that I have my additional information from Peta, is her feeling expressed in the first tape that, 'when my father died . . . there wasn't any longer a chance to grow into another kind of relationship with him'. And later, 'I hated him for dying, sure as hell, I was very angry'. Then, 'it pains me that men I respect turn away from me so soon'. This later pain surely has echoes from the time of her father's death. I wish to explore the ramifications of this. There are other strong feelings too: fear, being bullied, an impulse to withdraw, being bored, and sometimes a sickening sense of isolation. I suspect, too, that there is a considerable amount of self-blame.

At one point Peta begins to talk about the phrase that popped into her head, 'mothers get blamed'. Some of the feelings about her mother may have been censored. The phrase makes me think uncomfortably of what Alice Miller (1990: 77) suggests, that 'some feminists don't care to listen to such questions' about the role of the mother.

I respect Peta's honesty when she says that 'the unspeakable fury of deprivation still assails me sometimes'. I also have noted and respect what she says in the beginning, that 'I am generally speaking a happy and contented individual who has much joy – I have much joy in my life'. It is eminently possible for someone to feel this, despite being aware of areas of alienation within themselves.

After reading and trying to digest what Peta has to say, I decided to write my questions in the form of a handwritten letter. I began by introducing myself. I generally say a little about myself and my way of working, but not in the detail which I offered in the letter. I was conscious of what a strange situation we were all in. Without an actual meeting there were aspects of what we were doing which could be experienced as mouthing into the air. Increasingly, therapists themselves and user movements encourage potential clients to ask questions before beginning therapy. Many of my clients have no prior knowledge of therapy or its culture. Explanations at the beginning often seem to bode well for them.

Some of what I asked Peta to consider in my letter now seem a little strange, particularly my questions about what she remembered from the time before her brother was born. I was fishing for an early sense of herself, and possibly an early sense of play. From her response to these questions, and her thoughts about screaming into a cushion, she is quite clearly telling me that I had no business asking about such things outside the confines of a therapeutic relationship. She is right. Nevertheless, some questions in the early stages of meeting a client are a little strange (on the therapist's part). Such questions, and how they are responded to, are part of the process of two human beings beginning to have a sense of one another. First meetings between people in any setting often contain a certain necessary awkwardness.

I reproduce the letter I sent, because it includes some of what I feel to be necessary explanations of the process of art therapy:

Dear Peta,
It is interesting to read your story and to begin a conversation with you which will take place over two years. Firstly, I would like to offer you a little information about myself and about my way of working. I am a woman. I have been working as an art therapist with the clients of the NHS Psychiatric Services for fifteen years. I also teach art therapy students who are training at the University of Sheffield. I have been teaching for ten years, having helped to initiate the training course in 1983. I continue to work both with the clients of psychiatric services and to teach students. Some of the clients with whom I work have serious psychotic disorders and some have a range of emotional difficulties, which are serious but not outside the range of what is understandable for most people. The work I do with people is long term for those who have psychotic disorders, and more brief for those who do not – the length of time offered to people does not always reflect what is needed but rather the pressure on health service time and resources.

Very simply I think of the work that I do as involving a three-way relationship between the client, the client's art work and myself. I do not read a client's art work like so many tea leaves (one understandable fear) but try to engage in an exploration of it alongside the client. A dreamer dreams their own dreams and we are in the end reliant on the dreamer to help us explore the world of the dream. I think it is the same with a client's art work. Something else which I think is important is the client's own sense of the need for exploration and change.

I would like to acknowledge and respect what you say generally speaking about being a 'happy and contented individual who has much joy'. My understanding so far of the feeling which you wish to lay to rest is one of pain and estrangement evoked by some significant men and some facilitators. You wish to address this feeling both for your own sake and because you wish to behave responsibly in relation to your training as a counsellor.

I was pleased to hear that you are familiar with making art, because predictably I would like you to try making some art work for yourself during the months of May and June. I would like to see some of this art work if possible, but what is most important is that you develop a relationship with your art work. It may be that your art work could help expand the internal dialogue you have already begun about the source of your pain.

Because you have been an art teacher it may seem impertinent to make suggestions to you which might help you begin the process of making art. I will tell you what I suggest to people who are less familiar with the art-making process – please simply take what is helpful and leave what is not. I suggest that people find a room or a place in a corner of a room which can become your place for reflection and reverie. Find things that you think you will need and make them ready, for example a table, some paints, collage or sculpting materials. Perhaps put up some old photos of your family, put posters on the wall, perhaps you want a radio or a tape-recorder or tea-making things ... Create your own setting and then allocate some time for yourself (one or two hour slots of time at regular intervals).

Some people find it helpful to begin to keep a journal and a scrapbook. This can be an entirely private place in which you can record thoughts and feelings which come to you about anything at all. The idea is not simply to write, but make pictures either by drawing or painting or using collage materials. You might want to include poems, your own or by others – equally you might find a passage in a novel or a magazine which seems relevant. All these things can help you in continuing your own internal dialogue – possibly one of the themes in the work of the scrapbook could be the 'gender agenda'; other themes to explore could be to do with feelings of boredom. The actual subject matter is, of course, up to you – but try to make the journal a place where you bring your feelings into the foreground.

The pictures I would like you to attempt are concerned with your life before your brother was born. Firstly, I would like you to try to remember how you used to paint and draw as a young child – maybe there were houses, ways of representing people and animals. For me, because I came from Hull, there were ships which I used to draw in a very particular way – maybe for you there are things you remember drawing on the houseboat. I would like you to draw some of these pictures again in the manner of a child.

Next, I would like you to adopt the same child's view (though not necessarily the style) and make two portraits, one of your mother and one of your father as you used to see them. Remember you can use any materials you wish, to suggest how you saw your mother and father when you were a child. Perhaps you could write to me briefly about how it feels making these portraits, and if you can include some words (say three for each parent) which you would have used as a child to describe their different personalities.

Finally, I would like you to make a picture of yourself as a child and again for you to write and introduce me to the little girl who used to live on a houseboat. If you can try to think about how you were the child of your parents' union.

In asking you to do all these things I am asking you to look back into the roots of your alienations in simple emotional terms. One example of how interesting an inquiry this could be might be for you to take some time to reflect on what the simple emotional roots of your feminism might be.

Good luck with all of this. I look forward to hearing from you.

Chris Wood

In response, and through a further meeting with Moira, Peta sent me a lot more material to consider. She also sent me two essays (concerned with gender issues in human development and in counselling), several pages of 'childhood notes', some poetry collected over several years, four pencil drawings, and one in ink. I was very interested to receive all this material. What initially leapt out at me was towards the end of the transcript of the conversation between Peta and Moira about my questions:

I don't understand why [my parents] stayed together, and in fact when I was sixteen – I'm sure I must have mentioned this, because it was such a hell of a big deal for me – my mother went to an international conference, met an American and fell in love, came back and a few months later, announced that she was going to move to America, take my brother with her because he was seven, and I was going to stay in England and live with my father. [*Pauses.*] And I was just so pissed off.

I remembered what had been said in the first session, also towards the end, which seemed a similarly important feeling of exclusion:

But that was really difficult: here was I, and my brother was play-fighting with my father. He was five, let's say, and I was at a stage, nine years older [*she speaks very slowly*], when I needed something. I certainly needed attention [*there is a long pause*], which I never got.

Space forbids reproduction of the whole of this second transcript, which seems to provide rich evidence of the need for a relationship in the therapy. In my assessment, I can only include those parts that seem to be most enlightening. I also reproduce the line drawings. I have included a few sentences from what Peta calls 'childhood notes'.

Assessment

The art work, the language and the writing which clients bring to art therapists, are central to the therapy. It is through all of these that a therapist finds her way of understanding the form of a client's feeling. The early stages might be said to involve a period of gazing at the material alongside the client. Schaverien has suggested that this stage of the work involves a process of identification. I invite the reader to gaze with me alongside Peta at the material she presented.

Peta commented on my letter: 'She tells me about her, which I found . . . self-disclosure's terribly useful to a person like myself. I value it enormously'. It is perhaps true for everyone that a little information about the therapist helps them feel a sense of inclusion. For Peta it seems to me that a sense of inclusion gives her the hope that equality and respect will be possible. She went on:

> She says, 'My understanding so far of the feeling which you wish to lay to rest is one of pain and estrangement evoked by some significant men and some facilitators'. That's not present time . . . Pain and estrangement is something I can sometimes get back to; and because of the experience has helped me in the work with clients. So . . . isn't it interesting that one should make such growth and progress in certainly a year ago, when we made the first tape?

It is good to hear that Peta has a sense of her growth and progress. The sense of her own power and strength might be something I focus upon at times. Nevertheless, it is not quite clear whether her pain has receded, or whether she has actually faced the feelings involved so that they have been much better digested.

I suggested she might want to include poems, which she did:

Love of Solitude
'I love being alone!
I love being alone!'
Defending herself from the night,
the hostess bangs her fist upon the table.
Oh dearest lady, what troubles you?
In this cry the soul is stripped naked.
People love solitude out of pain,

Never out of joy!
Solitude brings silence
Which spares us from insult.
Solitude means no offense.
Solitude understands
As a man cannot understand.
Solitude can embrace
As a man cannot embrace.
But the dress is worn on bare
Nerves
and all its hooks are red-hot!
'I love being alone!' is to shout
'It doesn't hurt' under torture.
But it does hurt
Lord how it hurts,
So that one wishes to hug at least somebody.
Solitude: the more it is hated,
the stronger the love.
One should raise a monument
to a woman's pain during her lifetime,
So that she could stand there
Reproaching men, stand there for ever.
'I love being alone!' And then whisper
the translation: a defenceless 'Don't go!'.

It is not clear to me whether or not Peta wrote this herself, or edited one written by someone else. The poem speaks powerfully for itself. I can understand that this may well describe some of the different layers of what she feels. I suspect the reproach the poem expresses is more strongly aimed at herself than at any one man, except perhaps her father.

The remaining poems which Peta offered me, are all (except the ideas on love by Vincent Van Gogh) clear expressions of the stab of pain which she sometimes feels. However, I think Peta expects me to understand that this is not all she feels:

Is that, my friend smiled, where you
Have your roots?
No, only where my childhood was
unspent,
I wanted to retort,
Just where I started from.

(*Not my poem, author unknown to me.*)

The best way to love God is to love many things. Love a friend, a wife something, what you like. But one must love with a lofty and serious intimate sympathy, with strength, with intelligence.

(Vincent Van Gogh)

Imagine yourself alone in the world, in the midst of nothingness and then try to tell me how large you are.

He who laughs
Has not yet heard
The terrible tidings.

Ah what an age it is
When to speak of trees is almost a crime
For it is a kind of silence about injustice!
And he who walks calmly across the street,
Is he not out of reach of his friends
In trouble?
It is true: I earn my living
But believe me, it is only an accident.

Peta comments: 'All these poems were collected by me in a commonplace book which I started in 1967'.

In place of my suggestion of a scrapbook for a gender agenda, Peta said: 'I shifted so much because of Chodorow and the other stuff. You see, I did this . . . in fact it might be helpful. I'll just offer this'. 'This' was the essays. I am curious about which parts of Nancy Chodorow's work have helped her over the last few months. Has she had some helpful thoughts about the gender-rearing influences in her original family, or perhaps in relation to her own son? Or could it be connected with discovering a vital sense of autonomy. I read Peta's essays with real interest. They did not do a great deal to enlighten me about the specific simple emotional roots of her experience. Nevertheless, their inclusion seemed a positive indication of her desire to make a relationship and to be understood.

Of the essays she says: 'I wrote one, handed it in, and it was thrown straight back. "This is not what we want, do it again please". I kind of knew it anyway. But I sort of had a rant, a sort of fit really. And then I did another one and I got 65%, so that's all right. I was really very pleased'. I suspect that having the first essay returned and rejected, and the second essay applauded touched on very deep specific feelings for Peta – very simply on her fear of rejection and on her joy and surprise at favoured inclusion.

In fact, I had suggested a journal which might be a 'scrapbook' for thoughts, feelings and images, a place to record her own internal dialogue, which might have the gender agenda as one of the themes. I will have to make the scope of a journal much clearer. Because of the range of material Peta has sent me – the poems, the childhood notes, the images, the essays – I think she understands very well the process of recording internal dialogue. In asking her to bring some of it together in one place, I want her really to focus on what she feels.

Peta commented on the journal and the drawings:

> She writes, 'Other themes to explore could be to do with the feeling of boredom'. Yes, that's a kind of sick feeling. A mixture of frustration and things of that sort. She says, 'The actual subject matter is of course up to you, but try to make the journal a place . . . '. I haven't done that actually. 'The pictures I would like you to attempt are concerned with your life before your brother was born'. Again I can't do it. Well, you have what I managed. She's taken such trouble to think . . . about the work that is in front of her here. But I have not actually been able to respond in quite the ways she says.

Moira then asked Peta if she could tell me about what got in the way of doing it? She replied:

> Yes. 'Your life before your brother was born' is this bit which . . . I can't, I can't get to. Partly because I would cry a lot, that's OK, but . . . there must be an awful lot of anger, you see, not being able to remember. I just can't do it. I could do it . . . probably. But I'd have to have a cushion to scream into.

Peta sent me instead a page of preliminary workings out (see Fig. 8), but the way I had asked for them had not actually enabled her to begin to make pictures about these areas. At this point, I wonder what sort of transference feelings might be there for me already – as an art therapist, a tutor and a possible authority figure who is not being helpful. Thoughts about transference feelings in these circumstances are necessarily very tentative. Asking about her sense of self before her brother was born is a lot to ask at a first encounter. I wanted her to think about an early sense of her self and hopefully remember early play. Peta thought that the emotions she would touch upon in doing this would be very powerful. Elsewhere she uses the phrase, 'I'd have to haul it in like a boat on a long painter, and it would take some time'. The idea of her needing a cushion to scream makes me feel more than a little wry about the process of long-distance encounter we are engaged in. What she needs and I think she has a clear instinct about, is not really a cushion, but a

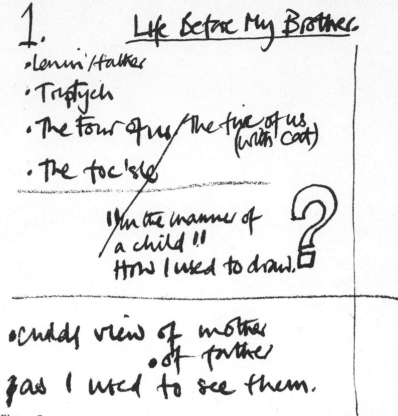

Figure 8

relationship that will help the screaming feel bearable.

I had asked Peta to draw as a young child. She showed Moira the drawing of her boat (see Fig. 9), commenting:

> And it's very interesting: she says 'in the manner of a child'. I think I've done this. This is the boat. This a diagrammatic . . . this is the wheel house, this is where my mother stood, this is the afterdeck where you could put chairs actually, this is the fo'c'sle where my cabin was, and this is the galley. Fifty-two foot it was, converted trawler, teak hull, diesel engine. Don't know what horse power it was, but I like diesel engines even now: they roar nicely. So this is all I can get 'in the manner of a child'.

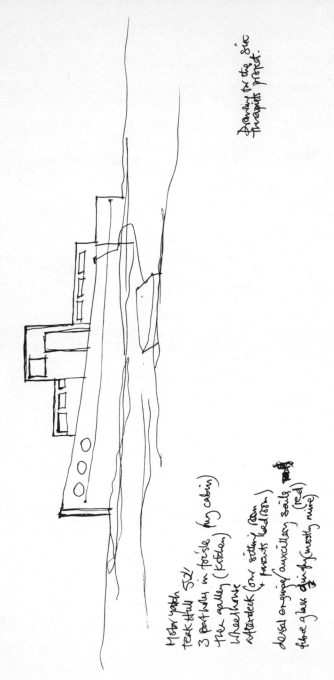

Figure 9

I would wish her to try some more pictures of the boat and the fo'c'sle, because I think quite a lot of her sense of self might have originated from that time. I am interested in her liking the noise of the diesel, the sense of safety in the fo'c'sle cabin, and (in her 'childhood notes') a reference to her father having to duck to get in the fo'c'sle cabin. The main drawing of the boat does indeed seem diagrammatic and a bit bleak, although there is something more alive and perky about the small boat, which in her 'childhood notes' she called 'the boatdweller's bike'. The picture looks to me like one that could have been made by an adolescent. I wonder if Peta might be able to fish for any earlier versions of it.

My letter also asked her to adopt the same child's view, but not necessarily style, and make a portrait of her mother and father as she used to see them. Peta said to Moira, in a whisper: 'I couldn't do it. Such a sensible thing to ask for a decent art therapist. "Remember how you can use any material . . . ".'

I really felt my guts twist in sympathy at her feeling unable to make these portraits. I began to wonder again whether this long-distance work was really wise. I comfort myself with the knowledge that the editors have undertaken to take good care of the clients who participated in the project. It would not have been possible to do any of this without that undertaking. Also in particular I suspect that Peta has quite strong feelings of positive regard for Moira because she quotes her often in her essays.

Moira asked Peta: 'What happened when you tried to?' She replied:

I panicked, I block . . . and 'Oh shit!'. And my father was very broad, and I was very small, and . . . give her that photograph thing. [Sighs.] Almost as if I was saying to myself, 'OK, if you want me to do this, I've got to have you here'. And I know you could do this work with me, and I know I could do it, and something would be done here, but I can't . . . do it alone.

In fact, Peta sent me three other drawings. Those I have called 'The Broad Man' (Fig. 10) and 'Father with Jug' (Fig. 11) are both portraits. The 'broad' picture I suspect is her father as she saw him as a child (although she does not really indicate this). If it is, her father looks huge – like a man in the rock? A child could nestle in those arms, but does the face look vacant, bleak like the boat in Fig. 9? It is crazy to speculate too much without Peta to refer to. I need her own thoughts to make any further exploration of the images with her.

One of the drawings in Fig. 11 is of her father, but it also contains quite a strong reference to her mother with the jug, which she

Figure 10

explains on the picture. The face looks kindly enough but the smooth-ness, the whiteness of the paper and the lack of pupils in the eye give the image a mask-like quality. I might ask her to work a little more on these pictures about her mother and father. She could perhaps do some pictures or paintings or claywork about the jug alone.

The act of drawing the childhood sculpture, on the right-hand side of Fig. 11, must have evoked all manner of feelings that I need to ask her about. It appears to be a huge man with a pleasing form, absorbed in reading. I wonder what it felt like looking at him when she was a child. I was rather puzzled that there was no clear reference in the second interview to these pictures. Instead, she described to Moira, using the image of a boat, how difficult she feared facing her feelings might be if she were to draw them:

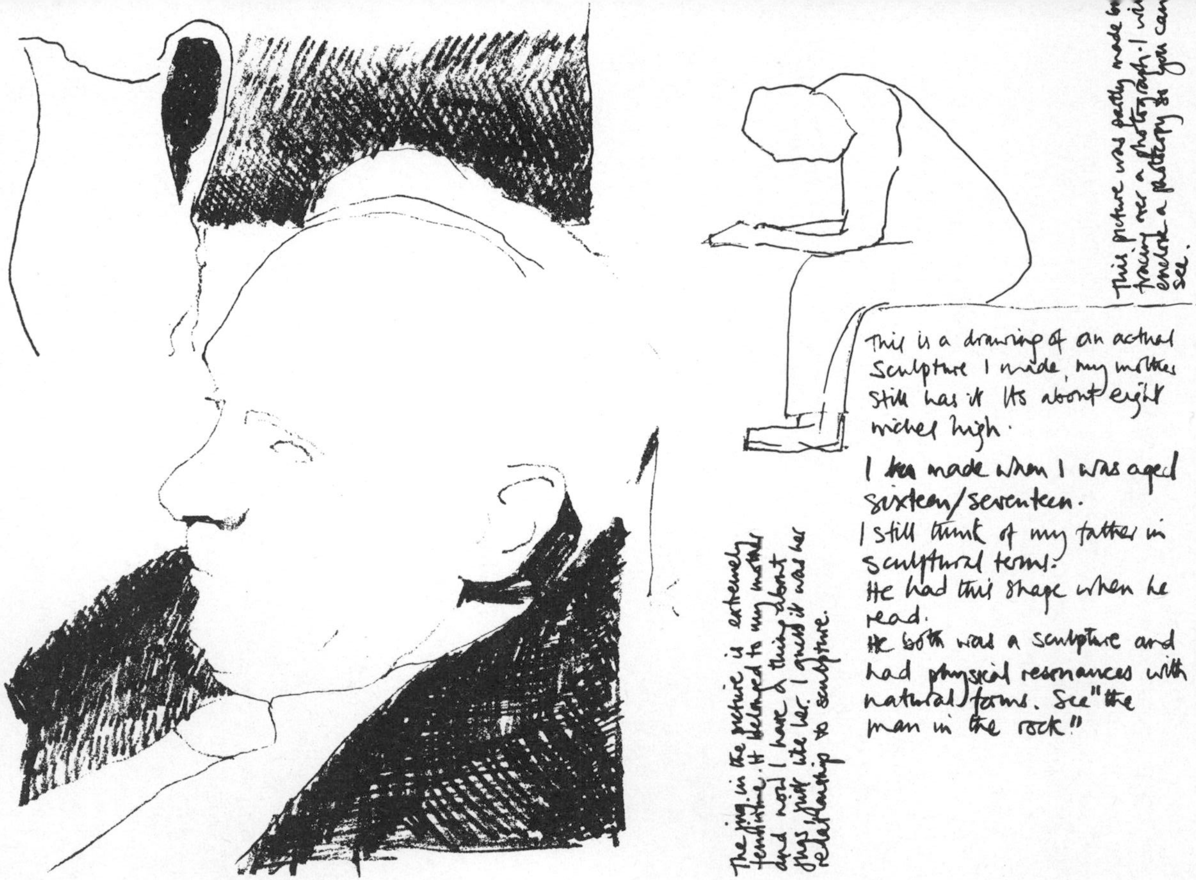
This picture was partly made
tracing over a photograph. I
enclose a photocopy so you can
see.
This is a drawing of an actual sculpture I made, my mother still has it. Its about eight inches high.
I made when I was aged sixteen/seventeen.
I still think of my father in sculptural terms.
He had this shape when he read.
He both was a sculpture and had physical resonances with natural forms. See "the man in the rock"
The jug in the picture is extremely tentative. It belonged to my mother and now I have a thing about jugs, just like her. I guess it was her relationship to sculpture.

Figure 11

I think it's so – I'd have to haul it in, like a boat on a long painter, and it would take some time. It's not because the boat's heavy, because it's on water, and you can do it all right. Then I know I'm on land, and I know that the boat is not leaking or anything, and I know it's sort of sound and everything, but it feels like a long rope, and maybe the tide's pulling the boat, and it's quite a light boat anyway and maybe the current's taking it. I'm quite capable of pulling and I'm strong enough to do it, and . . . oh [*feigns a groan*].

Finally, I had asked Peta to make a picture of herself as a child, to write and introduce me to the little girl who used to live on a houseboat, and to think about how she was the child of her parents' union. I refer again to her words at this point in the second interview, because they seem very important:

And I found out why my mother fell in love with my father, because he was of course stunningly good-looking. I don't understand why they stayed together, and in fact when I was sixteen – I'm sure I must have mentioned this, because it was such a hell of a big deal for me. My mother went to an international conference, met an American and fell in love, came back and a few months later, announced that she was going to move to America, take my brother with her because he was seven, and I was going to stay in England and live with my father. [*Pauses.*] And I was just so pissed off.

The last phrase covers what must have been a biting and confusing feeling of rejection. Her mother was apparently saying that she did not want Peta. Her father died before she had the chance to get to know him. Perhaps Peta drew the conclusion that it is better to withdraw and suffer feelings of exclusion rather than risk rejection.

Of the picture she drew in response to my request (Fig. 12), Peta said: 'So she asks for the picture of myself as a child, I can't do. But I draw a cat, with a girl child somewhere but I wouldn't be gendered'. Although Peta says she cannot do a picture, there is a picture. I cannot read a lot into it. Is it an ungendered child in an uncomfortable life jacket?

In my letter, I asked Peta to look back into the roots of her alienation. She gives an account of a slow dawning sexuality, which suggests quite strongly to me that she had withdrawn from that aspect of herself in her late teens and early twenties. Her overall sense of herself at that time cannot have been very substantial:

Actually because she's good, this woman, I am able to access some of it in simple emotional terms. I think I've managed

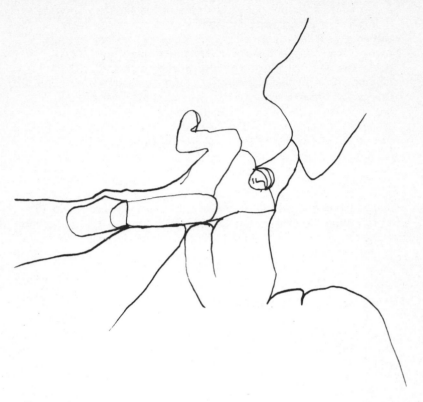

Figure 12

to look at some of the roots. One example of how
interesting an enquiry this could be . . . 'Simple emotional
roots of feminism'. My feminism, yes. Oh God! I mean, I
was raised a Socialist, I've been a life-long Socialist, and that
probably will . . . always, philosophically a Socialist as well as
politically. I'm a very Utopian Socialist. My parents talked
about Mandela and South Africa from very early on. Little
things, all the time. I was apparently named after some
Korean hero, some bod did something heroic. They
eventually divided the country. But something to do with
the persecution of Communist heroes. I embraced feminism
as many women did at the time – it was a tremendously
important time. The importance of it was that it was both a
highly individual . . . that was what was so exciting about it.

It was both a terribly personal thing and it was also about half of all of us humans, and has profoundly shaped my thinking as it has many women's. In fact I was reading last night a book on art history where the woman says, 'This book, I wrote it as a result of the women's liberation movement'. And many women . . . I am earnestly longing, in the sort of Quaker sense of desiring, earnestly waiting and desiring, and waiting in almost that sort of spiritual sense, for another rising up of that collective consciousness, the sort of thing I was part of . . . for young women . . . because it's supported and given such a strong foundation.

I think Peta's enthusiasm and earnest desiring of another rising up of collective consciousness is because the feminist movement ('because it's supported and given such a strong foundation') has given her a sense of belonging and significance, in a way which her parents did not manage.

Therapeutic possibilities

The sheer wealth of Peta's material (only some of which I have included here) suggests that she is familiar with exploring her own internal dialogue. This familiarity can be used to help her. She seems to have good instincts about needing a relationship for therapy, and this bodes well.

Judging from her wide-ranging use of this material, I do not think there are any contra-indications to the use of art therapy for Peta. Sometimes when people are familiar with art-making processes, they become very self-conscious in using their art in therapy – they can become like people thinking about how they walk, who fall over and cannot walk for thinking about it. I do not think this would occur with Peta, although I wonder what has happened to her use of art during her adult life – she does not say anything about this. It may be that she needs to rouse that side of herself from sleep. Of course I cannot know about this, I can only speculate.

The art in the therapy may be for Peta a good way of interrupting any impulse to withdraw or fly from difficult feelings. From all that she has shared about herself, I wonder if the art she makes might help her to explore her fear of rejection and exclusion within the boundaries of the therapy relationship. Sometimes a stronger sense of self can emerge as a result of dedicated use of art and the play it involves, even though it may sometimes feel frightening.

The course of therapy

The art work which I would encourage Peta to make, and her relationship with me, cannot be predicted in advance. I think it will be possible to help her focus on those issues and feelings which she needs to explore. No therapeutic method is a panacea, but if Peta wished to commit herself to a relationship with me and if I could help her focus on what she feels, something very useful may happen.

Where possible, the meetings I arrange with her will be held at the same time and place each week, with clear time limits. These deceptively simple boundaries of time and place provide therapeutic relationships with a strong enough framework within which to undertake the emotional exploration. They can help both the therapist to be steady enough and the client to feel safe enough. The length of individual sessions is a little longer than in other therapies based on talking alone: a session might be for one hour and fifteen minutes as opposed to one hour, in order to give Peta enough time to make some art work: 'To control what is outside one has to do things, not simply to think or to wish and doing things takes time. Playing is doing' (Winnicott 1971: 47).

My instinct is to offer Peta focused, time-limited work: weekly meetings for a three-month period, then a review of the situation with her, with the possibility of an extension for a further three months if that seems appropriate to both of us. My instinct about offering time-limited work is connected to a feeling that Peta could use it as a way of helping herself focus on what she feels. She is quite practised at flying away from what she feels into intellectual explanations, which she herself acknowledges: 'because I'm rather widely read on certain aspects of feminism I can be drawn into a kind of sociopolitical analysis of why I feel threatened by men'. I suspect she might be very good at diverting her attention away from her feelings – of course, most of us need help with this at times.

I wish to respect her sense that 'I am generally speaking a happy and contented individual who has much joy – I have much joy in my life'. I have the impression that those feelings which she wishes to lay to rest are not all encompassing, although they are deep-rooted.

The room in which I would work with Peta is an art studio. It is not quite right to suggest that such rooms are like playrooms for adults, but there is something of that in them. I hope to make the room inviting, a place where it is possible to daydream and explore using the art materials. Clients need help to find the space inside themselves and in their lives in order to begin to make some art work, and in order to make something happen in their lives. Estés

(1992: 299) writes about the necessity of making space for one's self: 'In archetypal lore there is the idea that if one prepares a special psychic place, the being, the creative force, the soul source will hear of it, sense its way to it, and inhabit that place'.

I would talk to Peta about making space in her life and of using the art room when she is with me, as a way of helping her to kindle some art work, whether pictures or writing. She seems to have an ability to use both. I might encourage her to find some stories which appeal to her whether they be fairy stories, myths, epic tales, detective stories or comic strips. I might encourage her to write some of her own. I would certainly ask her to use some of the time spent with me drawing and painting. It seems that Peta had difficulty working visually in 'the manner of a child'. I need to talk to her about this: maybe it is not helpful to pursue this. I am interested in her name – a pseudonym but probably one which bears some of the same gender ambivalence, since she was given the name of a war hero. Making some images about her name and its associations for her may be a way of helping her to begin working with me. There are many themes in her story as she has told it, which it may be helpful to explore further. Once she begins, I will follow where her art work leads us – while being aware myself of the time available and of the need to help Peta focus on what it is she feels.

I have already said how struck I was by Peta's difficulty in making some of the pictures which I initially asked her to try on her own. She herself felt very strongly that she needed to do them in the presence of a relationship. Her relationship with Moira, although I suspect a good one with some aspects of therapy in it, clearly has a function which is different from a therapeutic one. Regularity and frequency of meetings with a therapist would enable a greater sense of safety to develop. Peta may then once again be able to feel that she is 'tied to the mast' in the way she described in her 'childhood notes': 'On a rough trip once my parents tied me to the mast. I remember feeling very confident at the time because I never felt pressure on the rope'. The element that is different in art therapy is clearly the inclusion of art. What Winnicott has to say about play is enormously relevant to what happens when someone is making art within a therapeutic relationship:

> The thing about playing is always the precariousness of the interplay of personal psychic reality and the experience of control of actual objects. This is the precariousness of magic itself, magic that arises in intimacy in a relationship that is being found to be reliable . . . When a patient cannot play the therapist must attend to this major symptom before interpreting fragments

of behaviour. The next stage is being alone in the presence of someone.

(Winnicott 1971: 55)

To be 'alone' in the presence of someone can be healing. The quiet presence of another can make it feel safer to reflect upon the self. Winnicott (1971: 55) continues that such playing is 'on the basis of the assumption that the person who loves and who is therefore reliable is available and continues to be available when remembered after being forgotten'.

The important areas that have emerged in Peta are fear of rejection and feelings of exclusion and their history in both her early relationship and in her teenage relationship with her mother and father. By her own account, these have led her to act upon the impulse to withdraw (possibly prematurely) from a number of situations. An actual therapeutic relationship with one therapist as opposed to a glancing encounter with six therapists might enable her to feel sufficiently secured 'to a mast' to contain her feelings. The quality and nuance of them can only be speculated about. However, I feel relatively confident that if Peta can really engage in the process of art making within the relative safety of a therapeutic relationship, it is extremely likely that her art work will touch upon the emotions it is most pertinent to explore, giving form to the feelings she needs to elaborate and recognize.

Schaverien has very helpfully suggested a series of processes which appear during a client's relationship with her art work: identification, familiarization, acknowledgement, assimulation and disposal. Of these stages she writes:

> . . . all involve active participation of the therapist. However, this activity may appear passive: her or his role is mainly one of 'holding'. The role is a response to the stage of the relationship of a client to her or his picture. Thus in the stages of identification and familiarisation, the therapist will accompany the client in viewing the pictures. She or he will observe the effect the picture has on the client and may even use this observation to make a comment. This is different from entering in to the picture in an intrusive manner.
>
> (Schaverien 1992: 106)

I am concerned as an art therapist to help the client to really listen to and see what they feel. Hobson, in *Forms of Feeling*, writes much that is helpful in thinking about the forms which feelings can assume. I identify with what he describes as the task of the therapist: 'not to explain but to attend; to remain in touch with and value what will emerge and lead forward' (Hobson 1985: 34–5).

Both the art-making process and the relationship with me can help in facing and feeling emotions. The idea of a triangular relationship within the process of art therapy is one which has been explored more thoroughly in recent years. Schaverien speaks of the relationship between the client, her art and the therapist as being charged, because the transference feelings which emerge can be experienced through the therapeutic relationship and through the dimension of the art work.

Problem areas

It is hard to know without meeting whether or not Peta and I could work together. She may experience me and my style of working as one which she needs to subvert. Although the early signs seem favourable, and she is liberal with her compliments of me, these could be followed by disappointment. Sometimes she has a tendency to say things are wonderful when actually they may not feel wonderful to her – her mother's relationship with her brother, for example. In the absence of a real meeting, I can only speculate about what form and purpose transference feelings might take. If Peta could sustain a relationship with me, it might also at times produce the impulse to withdraw, which it might not be possible to prevent. She might feel too angry and upset to accept the necessary boundaries of a therapeutic relationship, although if this does happen it will not necessarily be a permanent condition.

Criteria for successful outcome

In an ideal world, a good outcome for therapy is when the client no longer feels the need for it. In the public sector, it is not often possible to offer open-ended work. With Peta there are specific reasons for offering time-limited work: it might help her to focus on what she feels. Sometimes a time limit can be counterproductive, in that the client may never feel safe enough to explore what she feels. With Peta I am hoping that a number of things will begin to happen. Initially, I want to do whatever I can to enable her to thoroughly engage with her art work. I do not know how difficult or how easy it will be for Peta to make space in her life (in the way Estés describes above) for this to happen. It is interesting what Schaverien has to say about the changes in the way the client engages with the art making:

. . . the preconceived picture in the 'mind's eye', is relinquished and so the form of expression changes; it gives way to purely symbolic expression. Thus the pictures are transformed from the diagrammatic to the embodied. The change is the result of the intensity of engagement of the client with the process . . . It is likely that the maker of the diagram is not engaged with the image making process, but nor is she or he engaged with the therapist as a person . . . The client who becomes engaged with the image making process is likely to become engaged with the therapist.

(Schaverien 1992: 102)

I am hoping that through the 'charged' process of engaging both with her art work and with me, it will become possible for Peta to realize where the problems lay in her childhood. This may be extremely painful work, but its fruit could be a genuine fading of her self-blame and her tendency to withdraw. The relationship and the art work could give her a place in which to voice the 'unspeakable fury' and the demand for inclusion and equality. Not all of this may be possible in a short time, but it might be possible for Peta to begin to feel more confidence in expressing and digesting difficult feelings. It is unlikely, judging from what she has shared, that the process will only involve feelings that are difficult and painful. Hopefully, part of it will engage that laughing part of Peta that likes to dress up cats in baby dolls' clothes or to roll on the floor with her son.

Summary

Patrick Casement (1990: 176) writes that the process of therapy can be enriching to both participants 'as true aliveness is rediscovered, as creativity is released from what had been blocking it and as patients recover the capacity to be more fully themselves and to be playful'. I hope it has been evident that art therapists put a lot of energy into the quality of attention they give to the language and the art work which their clients bring to them. This is done in order to try to pursue the form which feelings assume.

What Peta has gained from this project will have provided her with an unusual opportunity to learn about different therapies and their potential for her. I imagine that much of what she has learned through the project will be specifically useful on a supportive level. I hope so. However, in one sense, the vital element of therapy – the relationship – has been missing from this. Within a therapeutic relationship, it is possible to feel sufficiently emotionally held to do important emotional work. This holding enables conflicts to be relieved if not resolved. Peta herself seems to have a good instinct about the need for relationships (of all kinds). It is this that really bodes well for her.

Further reading

Bettelheim, B. (1989). *Freud and Man's Soul*. London: Penguin.

Bettelheim, B. and Rosenfeld, A.A. (1992). *The Art of the Obvious*. London: Thames and Hudson.

Casement, P. (1990). *Further Learning from the Patient: The Analytic Space and Process*. London: Tavistock/Routledge.

Estés, C.P. (1992). *Women Who Run with the Wolves: Contacting the Power of the Wild Woman*. London: Rider.

Hobson, R.F. (1985). *Forms of Feeling: The Heart of Psychotherapy*. London: Tavistock.

Miller, A. (1990). *Banished Knowledge: Facing Childhood Injuries*. London: Virago.

Phillips, A. (1993). *On Kissing, Tickling and Being Bored*. London: Faber and Faber.

Sayers, J. (1986). *Sexual Contradictions: Psychology, Psychoanalysis and Feminism*. London: Tavistock.

Schaverien, J. (1992) *The Revealing Image: Analytical Art, Psychotherapy Theory and Practice*. London: Routledge.

Winnicott, D.W. (1971). *Playing and Reality*. London: Tavistock.

10 REVIEW AND RESPONSE

Writing this chapter seems a long way from our starting point some years ago when we first played with the idea of this series. Much ground has been covered since, in this volume mostly by Peta. As I write this, it is over two years since she first considered participating. The process that followed has been a complex one for her. As our readers know from the opening chapter, Peta took considerable time to decide whether or not to participate. She decided to go ahead. She told me her story – perhaps the relatively straightforward part of this process – and I sent the transcript of it to the therapists. We waited for their questions.

I was very impressed with the care, thought and concern for Peta that all the therapists in their different modalities displayed. Having received all their questions, working on them with Peta was a lengthy and time-consuming task. Peta matched the commitment shown by the therapists with her own, giving considerable thought to her responses. Inevitably, sensitive and thought-provoking areas were touched on and Peta dealt with these with honesty and integrity. It was evident that many questions or comments were in themselves quite illuminating to her, opening up new ways of understanding and of perceiving herself and her situation. It was a fascinating part of the process to see how some therapists, even via myself as a third party, were able to make real connections with Peta. More is said about this below.

The therapists duly received the material they had requested and then came a long wait. It must have felt particularly long for Peta, as we waited for their chapters to arrive. It is an inevitable part of the process of publishing this type of book that it occurs in fits and starts. There is a burst of sustained work, then there is a lull while the busy activity continues elsewhere – in this instance with our therapists. So we sat and waited, while they thought and wrote. But the wait was undoubtedly more complex for Peta: it felt like my book, but it was a crucial part of her whole being.

Then the chapters started to arrive and copies were sent promptly to Peta. At this point, I was longing to know her response to them but did not make contact. As the reader will recall, we had agreed with our clients that we would be available to offer any support as and when needed and requested; that we would put them in contact with a therapist if they wished, but would not offer them therapy ourselves. As becomes clear in the account that follows, my decision to leave Peta to make contact if she wished, arising from my double desire to both keep to agreed boundaries and also not to invade her space and process, caused difficulties for her, although this was not known to me at the time.

The aim of this last chapter is to review with Peta, as the key player, the various contributions to this book. Peta and I had worked closely throughout on this project and it felt very important to work equally closely on this final stage. Prior to the first in this last series of meetings we had made telephone contact to arrange details of time and place. Peta had expressed some anxiety and worry about these final discussions. I, or so I genuinely thought, had responded in an appropriately reassuring and explanatory manner. This proved not to be the case. Quite unknowingly, I had entirely missed what she was really trying to communicate. This was a combination, I suspect, of my tiredness at the time resulting in insufficient sensitivity to the underlying nuances of her words, and of Peta being unable to clearly express what she needed (and readers may well identify here a theme in the book and wonder why I missed this at the time).

When we met, it was evident that Peta was very angry with me. Initially, we dropped all attempts to explore the material in the chapters. It was clearly crucial to enable her to express what she was feeling and to deal with the resulting issues between the two of us. Peta was feeling insufficiently supported and cared for by me at a point in the process where she was feeling somewhat bombarded. Her anger was on two levels: first, simply and directly at me; and second, at herself for not having said what she wanted. One part of her thought it was unfair to rage at me because I could not have known; another part felt that I just should have done. I correspondingly felt a mixture of emotions: deeply concerned that she should feel this way – looking after the client had been a genuine priority throughout; and, if I am honest, a little indignant myself, that I could not be expected to second guess. We spent considerable time working on and resolving this, until we both felt able to move on to our other discussions.

Both Peta and I wanted to include this aspect of the work in this chapter. We felt we had worked well and closely throughout and that we had a relationship that we valued. As in therapy, and all other relationships, negatives are ignored at their peril. We did not wish to sweep them under the carpet either between ourselves or in this book. In a project of this kind, real people are involved. Peta had very generously and bravely shared much of herself. The whole process gave her much, and real changes occurred as a result; as all clients know, change may be exhilarating, freeing and exciting, but it is also frightening and painful. Challenge can be thought-provoking and inspiring, but it can be overwhelming and alarming. It can be difficult in therapy to maintain this careful balance so that clients are not overwhelmed. In a project of this kind, it is especially problematic, and my thanks go to Peta for all her time, energy, enthusiasm and commitment. I also wish to acknowledge the pain that at times was the other side of the coin.

We spent many further hours in discussion related to this part of the book. What follows is an overview of the six contributions, incorporating Peta's own comments. Inevitably, she had more to say on some chapters than on others. It is obvious that with the range of approaches and people included in this volume, some made more sense to her or more connection with her, than did others. Peta was anxious that all the therapists were aware that this did not in any sense devalue those she responded to less. Sometimes this simply reflected her own individual preference. In other instances, when she had greater familiarity with an approach, this lessened its impact and correspondingly her responses. She was deeply moved by the efforts they had all made in working on, and responding to, her story. She felt valued and validated by many of their comments, although others had impact of a more problematic and painful nature. In commenting on each, the only significance in their ordering is that this is how Peta discussed them.

John Rowan

This was one of the contributions that had enormous impact on Peta. She responded to John Rowan very positively from the beginning, when his questions were put to her (although at this stage she did not know the names of any of the therapists). She continually referred to him as 'the decent man therapist', and felt warm towards him throughout. This was reflected in her spontaneously giving him material he had not asked for: finding photographs from childhood, and sending him poems and essays she thought he would find

informative. Receiving his chapter was powerful for her: 'It precipi-
tated me into a different mode of thinking and feeling. He's good
and he stirs up a lot of early stuff that are in my back files'.

We spoke about this chapter at length and her responses were not
only interesting but very informative. Her thoughts and responses
obviously have to be condensed throughout, but in essence she felt
that although John Rowan pinpoints very accurately areas of her
past that were indeed relevant and significant, nevertheless she would
not choose this approach. Essentially, she was saying, 'right person,
wrong approach'; and we both noted that perhaps the two aspects
need to feel sufficiently comfortable. To expand on this further, Peta
herself said:

> He was right but I wouldn't want to touch it [very early
> material]. It touched my mother being strapped down on a
> table when she had me. I have already visited it you see, and
> I don't want to go back to all that, and don't actually feel
> it's necessary. I don't need to go back to that to make things
> better now. He stirred something that was dangerous. It was
> rocky. It was very powerful, but I'd be cautious about this
> therapy. Others would be as effective but less dangerous. My
> gut feeling is, 'yes, there's something there, but no'. But he's
> very good.

It is obvious that what really jumped out at Peta was John Rowan's emphasis on early experiences. It is of course difficult to know
(as it is throughout) if Peta were really in therapy with John Rowan
whether he would be able to make it safe enough for her, particularly
as she had such genuinely positive and warm feelings towards him.
However, I was left feeling that no matter how careful the therapist
– and Rowan explains in his chapter the great care he takes to
ensure safety – she would be uneasy with this approach. It should
be noted that the very reservations that Peta expressed are in part
reflected in Rowan's own words, as he wonders if she would need
to avoid the pain of early traumas. For those people seeking therapy,
it is important to emphasize that it is absolutely valid for them to
trust their own sense of which therapeutic approach is most appropriate for them. Some therapists and therapies, while pinpoint-
ing problem areas accurately and sensitively, may not match either
what the client wants or can cope with.

Peta was very concerned that John Rowan would not feel attacked
or hurt by her comments, and she reiterated how she had valued his
chapter. She somewhat tentatively raised a point relating to whether
men should work with birth material with women clients. We had
a lengthy discussion on this. We failed to reach any conclusions,

but thought our readers might be interested in the gist of the conversation. Peta wondered how much the whole birth experience for women, whether in giving birth themselves, or having been given birth to, was something only other women could truly empathize with. She wondered if a man could get inside this experience sufficiently to understand the real quality and nature of women's feelings as they arise from these very crucial and early issues. Even in discussing this, we struggled to find words. At one point Peta commented, 'I haven't the words, but you sense absolutely what I mean, because you've been there too'. We became rather involved in this discussion, and I omitted to check whether not choosing this approach would have been any different if the therapist had been a woman. I suspect not. However, it is an interesting question to ponder.

John Rowan describes himself as a humanistic and integrative psychotherapist who in his work with clients likes to go back a long way. He emphasizes very early experiences in a way that is different from the other therapists in this book. Early trauma, the birth experience and even before that, are seen as both deeply significant and also as accessible to the client. He certainly uses many terms that are familiar to those who use analytic and dynamic approaches: defences, repression, the unconscious. Very early in his response to Peta he wonders about the importance of life before her brother, (as does Christine Wood) wondering if the memory of her brother's birth was a 'screen memory'. Although this latter is a term familiar to psychoanalytic psychotherapists, there are many examples of a very different use of terminology and approach to that of the other therapists. He discusses myth and counter-myth, and describes how he would use and work with dreams and fantasies, rather than staying solely on the level of 'prose consciousness'. Again some of this may also apply to the work of other therapists, but 'primal pain' and 'primal integration' – aimed at releasing the real self – are central concepts, and may be terms that are not familiar to every reader. They are certainly not used by the other contributors. As the term 'integrative' implies, this approach is a rich mixture, coming from diverse but complementary origins; the mixture reflects this therapist's extensive and diverse background and training.

In Rowan's questions to Peta he looks at key relationships in her life: her father, brother, mother and son. He picks up, as do several of the other therapists, the theme of silence. Interestingly, he does not mention her former husband, in common with most of the other therapists. He very much understands Peta's problems as not so much to do with men, but more to do with her whole way of being in the world. He is the only one of the therapists to redefine her difficulties in this way. He wonders how it would be for Peta working with a man, as does John Ormrod. And as we have seen, Peta had her own thoughts on this. He hopes she would see him as the good father she wanted. He acknowledges the care he would need to take not to reproduce her father's negative behaviours. However, he does not apparently consider that a negative transference could occur spontaneously, independent of, and unrelated to, his actual behaviour. It is not clear if this is an omission, or if he does not perceive the probability or possibility of negative transference in this way.

Peta clearly appreciated Rowan's awareness of the complexities for a woman bringing up a son in this culture, as she did his references to his grounding in feminism. She experienced this as being a present and intrinsic part of his approach. With regards to outcome, John Rowan predicts the process lasting about two years, wondering if Peta's training as a counsellor might impede the process. He acknowledges that there is a danger that *his* desired outcome – discovering her real self – might not be hers. However, he feels this outcome to be essential if she is to be enabled to make authentic choices. He will look for evidence of change in some improvement in her relationships, and notes that there had already been some changes with her brother. He also recognizes that in the end her mother may be particularly important. He draws attention to therapy occurring in phases, and makes an interesting comment on the gender question, thinking that different phases in therapy may need a different gender therapist. This possibility is also mentioned by Jennifer Mackewn, and perhaps links to Peta's own questions relating to early material and which gender therapist would be most appropriate for that work.

Jennifer Mackewn

This was the other contribution that made a particularly strong impact on Peta. She experienced Jennifer Mackewn as deeply communicative, and this was reflected in my experience of reading MacKewn's words to Peta, and asking Peta her questions. It felt as if she was in the room with Peta, whose responses were particularly vivid, spontaneous and alive. She readily and enthusiastically absorbed MacKewn's explanation of the Gestalt approach, and particularly liked the references to it being holistic. She appreciated both that Jennifer Mackewn explained her approach so carefully, and that she was prepared to offer some information about her herself. Peta felt strongly that she would find some self-disclosure helpful.

This latter point is particularly interesting: to Peta explanation and information about the therapist felt like an equalizing of the relationship. This was something she would value and it would assist the therapeutic process. Yet in some therapeutic approaches, such self-disclosure is almost anathema, even if others see this as a significant part of the process. It raises questions: How much is therapeutic technique in the interest of the client? How much is it a protection for the therapist? And, how much is it pure tradition that is simply never questioned? Peta's comments on these points may have a wider relevance and application, certainly with some clients.

Peta drew some interesting comparisons between her response to Jennifer Mackewn's chapter and the one by John Rowan. This reflected the impact both had made, although there were great differences in the particular form of this impact. Peta's own words expressed this most clearly as she described her reactions to receiving Jennifer MacKewn's chapter:

> I read it very quickly and read it again twice over slowly. I was really sitting up in my chair on the second reading. I had to put it down and come back to it after a cup of tea and think, 'Whew! She's right!' She's quite confrontational and she's rather strong, so in a way that is quite dangerous. But it's a different sort of danger [to John Rowan]; this one feels safe, and that one didn't. And that's very important.

She felt the difference was in their approach: as we have seen, Rowan stresses early life, Mackewn does not. She places considerably more emphasis on the present while stressing that she will not ignore Peta's past. She envisages that the past will emerge through paying close attention to the present. The starting point is *now* not *then*. This emphasis is obviously different and is one Peta herself mentioned, that the past will be accessed via a different route.

In reading Mackewn's account, it is evident that she will suggest that Peta try out specific activities. Again this is different from the other therapists, with the exception of John Ormrod, who also discusses both experimentation and homework assignments. I asked Peta to clarify how she felt about direct suggestions for action being made by the therapist, for instance experimenting in completing her sentences. This was her response:

> It felt great because I actually began to make experiments. It helped me take risks. She could both make contact and say things which were action-oriented, which were actually helpful. It's present time stuff, and it's breaking through language to action; and I'm actually very verbal, which can be a pain to me. And I can defend with words. Intervening in the present can help resolve past issues, it reaches into

them. It can be very activating, and cuts through old stuff. A
mixture of being fed by bits and challenged by bits, but it's
not threatening, although she's quite tough and really pins
things down. She's constructive, and she's engaging me in a
joint quest in which I feel I have an ally.

It is clear from Peta's own description that this therapist made
contact in such a way as to make both challenge and direct suggestions very acceptable. The latter would not have been possible
without the former. It is as if Peta and Jennifer Mackewn began to
form a relationship, although they had not met. Indeed, it is interesting to note that all the therapists, although they use somewhat
different language, see the formation and maintenance of a relationship as of primary importance. It is also significant that Peta felt
very safely held and contained by Mackewn, perceiving her both as
a strong and challenging therapist. Peta would have found any hint
of anxiety on the part of any therapist quite paralysing to her. Her
sense of ease with this particular therapist was further illustrated by
the alacrity with which she responded to the suggestion that she
might do some drawings. She did so spontaneously, with absorption
and without anxiety.

Peta also very much liked the language used by Mackewn. This
was evident in putting her original questions to Peta, but also as
Peta talked about reading the completed chapter. She described her
language as 'terribly rich, and so often spot on'. At this point, Peta
was referring to Mackewn's recognition and description of the themes
of isolation and withdrawal, and the circularity for Peta of needing
attention. Peta felt these were very accurately noted and discussed.
She also liked the way Jennifer Mackewn pondered on what she actually *meant* by the word 'subversive'. Peta responding by saying,
'*Yes*, you absolute love!' It felt as if this were tremendously important to her.

It will come as no surprise to the reader that although there were
several therapists Peta felt she could happily go to, Jennifer Mackewn
was the one who would be her first choice, because:

She did the most; she shifted the most; she actually enabled
me to go out and do things that I wasn't doing. I hadn't
had the nerve to ask for things I wanted and she helped me
to do that. I was able to do my own therapy.

In considering these last words, I am left thinking that it may be
particularly crucial for some clients to experience real external changes
quickly, while for others this may not be so. It raises the question
that some of our therapists ask regarding client expectations. It seems

that the combination of Jennifer Mackewn and Gestalt was the right person and the right approach for this particular client.

There are a few additional points arising from this account that merit attention. Mackewn works to a contract, albeit one that is flexible and negotiable. An interesting feature of this contract is the explicit attention paid to endings, which has a different emphasis from other approaches described here – although, as we shall see, John Ormrod is also aware of the importance of endings from the very start. Questions that arise relating to the significance of contracts to the client are discussed below.

Like John Rowan, Jennifer Mackewn has had a wide-ranging training. Although she later specialized in Gestalt, her comprehensive approach perhaps reflects her own diverse background as well as being, in her words, 'typical of the best Gestalt'. She takes great care to check out what Peta wants from therapy and whether her support systems are sufficient. She explains her own approach which, as we have seen, was well received by Peta. Both she and John Ormrod explore areas such as alcohol and drugs use, although they do so somewhat differently. Generally, she takes care to ensure that Peta can cope with the process. Another similarity between Jennifer Mackewn and John Ormrod is that they may both use formal diagnostic procedures, although Mackewn does so with reservations. As mentioned above, she invites Peta to draw. The only other therapist to do so is the art therapist. She also invites Peta to use visualization, although this technique is reminiscent of those referred to by Rowan.

I have already referred to Peta liking Mackewn's use of language. The theme of language in a different context is worth noting. In my comments on John Rowan's chapter, I mentioned that some of the terms he uses seemed to come straight from analytic theory. Similarly, some of the language used in Mackewn's chapter – terms such as 'resistance', 'introjection' and 'projection' – may come as a surprise to some readers in their inclusion under the Gestalt umbrella. Mackewn later points out that transference as a concept is not one Gestalt therapists object to; rather, they dislike an over-emphasis on the transferential relationship to the exclusion of other forms of relatedness. Of course, some therapists in the psychodynamic school – myself included – would agree. Yet at the same time terms are included (such as 'desensitization') which many associate with behavioural approaches, while 'confluence' and 'dialogic relationship' seem particular to this approach. Perhaps this may support Jennifer Mackewn's own comment that there are more similarities between approaches than many care to admit. Nevertheless, there are key differences in the two chapters I have examined so far, and approaching the client primarily through the past (Rowan) or through the present (Mackewn) is a prime example.

John Ormrod

Peta was anxious to explain that she had found John Ormrod's account interesting and that she appreciated – as she did with all the contributors – his thought, care and hard work on her behalf. However, she found it hard to give much feedback on his chapter; it was as if she had failed to engage with him. As she described it, the approach itself did not engage her, and therefore neither could the person. This is an interesting comment in the light of her responsiveness to Jennifer Mackewn: she had to feel a connection with her before her suggestions could be used. Although John Ormrod makes it clear that establishing a good therapeutic relationship is central, and he (like Mackewn) also explains the model of therapy, it was nevertheless not possible for Peta to locate him within it. It seems from what she had to say that because this was the wrong approach for her, the therapist somehow failed to get a look-in.

I wondered myself if he had disappeared with the completion of the questionnaire. Peta made no objection to the questionnaire itself; she filled it in quite obediently but without much interest. She responded far more to his questions put through me to her. It was clear that some of them were extremely pertinent and relevant, especially those relating to her father's death, to losses in general and to being bullied at school. It is not that Ormrod is failing to pick up important and relevant areas. He clearly is. It is rather that the style of work being offered, within which his questions are contained, are clearly not what she wants:

> The questionnaires were no problem: easy, just tick boxes.
> I've had experience of that, and I even remembered taking
> the eleven-plus, that was tick boxes. As I completed the
> questionnaires I thought, 'What on earth is this? This is
> nothing to do with me or anything else'. I didn't actually
> find that very helpful. It was all very interesting in one way
> but it didn't touch me. I feel it's a useful tool box but that it
> doesn't get near. It was absolutely remote from me. I have in
> the past argued myself out of depression, you know, with
> one of those books – 'How to Beat Depression' or some such
> thing. Real cognitive therapy; and I wouldn't want to enter
> that type of work.

It is of course interesting to note that Ormrod is working as a clinical psychologist within what remains of the NHS. The pressures on this service and others like it are to my knowledge huge. He comments himself that within the NHS Peta would be unlikely to be offered psychological help. It seems as if they have each turned the other down!

Ormrod, in common with several of the authors, discusses the commonalities between therapies, and does not want to be drawn into making falsely rigid distinctions. Nevertheless, in his approach, as with others, there are distinctions to be made that may be highly significant to the client. The use of pre-session questionnaires is an obvious one. As he explains, these fulfil several functions for the therapist: eliciting information, socializing clients into their role, and encouraging potential clients to begin to consider themselves and their problems. It appears that for Peta completion of a questionnaire would not have helped to socialize her as a client – rather the opposite. Instead of drawing her nearer to herself or her potential therapist, it actually distanced her. This begs the wider question of whether this approach, by its very nature, alienates some people from the start. I noted one very direct question on whether the client has been abused. I felt somewhat uneasy: I sensed a potential trap for clients. It assumes a willingness and ability to answer which may not be the case. And yet an initial answer to this question of 'no' may be difficult to undo at a later stage, when the client may be ready to reveal more. This could be the case with many of the other questions. But on the other side, the use of a questionnaire may be one way busy therapists in underfunded services have of working more quickly and effectively. Perhaps in that context the advantages of gathering information outweigh the disadvantages. Ormrod is the only therapist of the six to gather information in this way, and it is important to examine its possible implications. Some therapists obviously find it a useful tool, while others feel that when and how a client volunteers both information and feelings cannot be artificially imposed.

John Ormrod does much more, of course, than just administer a questionnaire, although this is the aspect that Peta was particularly influenced by. I have already noted the pertinence of some other areas he covers. What stands out in his approach is the clarity with which he perceives and explains the links between beliefs, the way the person structures the world, and their affect and behaviour. In this method, identifying and then disconfirming basic beliefs is a central focus.

This is essentially a focused approach to therapy which attempts to identify core beliefs, to trace links, to understand them and thereby to bring about change and the development of new skills. However, it also emphasizes the relationship between the client and the therapist: listening, empathizing and explaining the process. Peta's presenting problem of difficulties with men is accepted as the focus and is understood as having arisen from her early relationships, with later relationships having fed her present self-concepts. Thus the past is seen as significant in that it aids the understanding of existing problems; but the focus of the work is in the present. Like Mackewn, Ormrod's approach incorporates experimentation and the use of imagery, although it elicited a very different response from Peta. Role-play is also seen as a possible therapeutic tool, and again is not mentioned by the other therapists.

Like John Rowan, Ormrod is sensitive to the issue of Peta seeing a male therapist, although he also recognizes that there will be issues too if she sees a woman. He is clear that the 'gender agenda' must be kept to the forefront. Similarly, he recognizes the importance to Peta of her feminist perspective. Endings are seen as important and as this is a time-limited therapy, the ending will have been in sight from the beginning. Again this is very different from open-ended approaches or those in which contracts are negotiable, with the possibility of extending the time available. As I noted earlier, the reader may wish to question the impact of this upon the therapeutic work. If only time-limited work is offered, does this mean the client will not feel safe enough? And will the content of the therapy thereby be limited? Or, conversely, do time limits enable clients to work faster, because there is a sense of urgency and of time running out? Are time limits experienced as constricting and restricting? Or do they offer a safe boundary that encourages a therapeutic engagement?

Therapeutic goals are another aspect of Ormrod's approach. Here he is considerably more explicit than most others in this volume. These goals will be agreed upon and worked towards, and progress will be monitored weekly. This can be done 'informally' or by using rating sheets. An interesting point arises here in relation to initial assessment. If goals are set relatively early in the process, it assumes that the client's difficulties are accurately definable at that point. This may have implications for the type of client this approach suits best. Some therapists might argue that the nature of a client's difficulty often only evolves with time, and cannot be easily defined in this way at an early stage. The cognitive-behavioural approach would appear to argue to the contrary.

Maye Taylor

I had been able to send three of the chapters to Peta at the same time. It happened that they were all written by women, and in one way or another Peta identified them as feminists. Two of them, Maye Taylor and Judy Moore, explicitly stated they were. Peta perceived Chris Wood as a feminist too. Peta had some comments to make about all three of them, comparing them with the three therapists already described.

> Three feminist therapists in a row . . . It was amazing. A mainstream Rogerian, an art therapist, and a psychodynamic therapist. I found all three absolutely fascinating. I was familiar with the ground so I knew the territory, and in a way none of them touched me nearly as deeply as the primal therapist. But I was terribly glad to have the three feminists. They were all very warm, very validating. But apart from being a positive experience, it was actually strengthening. They were all very holding and containing and warming. Really I could have worked with any of them. They actually say things like, 'I like this woman', and that was terribly important, so therapeutically valuable. They made real contact even though they weren't there.

As the reader will note, this is reminiscent of Peta's comments on Jennifer Mackewn, although in that case this is more strongly in evidence. Peta continued:

> There *is* something different about the four women from the two men; but it's hard to say what it was and whether it's because they're women. Maybe they had an ability to empathetically get into the multifaceted business of how it is to be a woman: the way that women can only be understood in all their different bits and pieces – their roles; their different functions. Even if they try to resist those roles they're still somebody's wife, somebody's mother. That's all I can say, but there is something there. Although I really did like the 'decent man' [John Rowan] and the other man seemed very decent too – but his approach just didn't impact.

Taking these three women therapists individually, Peta was obviously impressed by Maye Taylor's responses. She liked her discussion of feminism, particularly her recognition that there are many forms this can take. She responded very positively to the theme of helping women to make choices and to understand the multiplicity of factors that are at work, as well as her recognition of the complexity of women's lives. Maye Taylor describes herself as a feminist psychodynamic psychotherapist. The centrality of this stance to her practice is both immediately clear and remains in evidence throughout her account. Historical factors and their influence on women are included in her initial description of herself. This recognition and incorporation of social history as well as individual history is strongly present. Although other therapists, for instance John Ormrod, refer briefly to societal factors, this is far away from an approach that establishes the significance of societal and political structures at its very core, while still holding the other focus of intrapsychic issues. To use Peta's own words to illustrate how she responded to this therapist:

> She's a very interesting person. I found her very wise. She's the kind of feminist that not only validates me as a feminist, but understands how difficult it can all be. She's affirming and I appreciate that. She feels strongly that it does matter that I'm a woman; and I like that because in actuality it gets rammed down my throat and there is no getting away from it.

Whereas other approaches have been aware of the significance of the gender of the therapist, the feminist position is perhaps the only approach where this is a core feature. In Taylor's chapter, the significance of gender is continually understood and worked with, both in terms of the relationship between the therapist and the client, and the client's relationship with the external world, and its impact on her inner world. To use Maye Taylor's adjective, gender forms a 'substantive' part of the relationship. This resonated powerfully with Peta's experience of being in the world as a woman. She was comfortable with this approach and felt that in an essential way it matched both the reality of her world and her understanding of it. The clear acknowledgement and belief that patriarchal society has a lot to answer for in relation to creating and maintaining women's distress, expressed lucidly by Taylor, was a theme that was deeply meaningful to Peta.

Peta also responded favourably to what she saw as Taylor's 'thoroughness'. She commented:

> She actually spends a lot of time pushing and pulling the dialogue backwards and forwards in a very detailed and careful way. There is great attention to detail and I very much appreciate that. She's really excellent. She gets hold of things too, so her comments aren't always comfortable but she makes me feel quite safe with her to look at difficult areas.

This last comment was important. Maye Taylor herself discusses at some length the fact that the process might be uncomfortable and painful. She is anxious to challenge and dismantle the myth that feminist therapy is cosy and collusive. She recognizes and states that painful areas lie ahead and acknowledges that viewing the personal as political does not lessen personal pain. She places a greater emphasis on working with Peta's rage than the others, and wonders if one risk for Peta might be leaving therapy even angrier than ever. Maye Taylor identifies Peta's rage as an almost inevitable consequence of the lives of working women. However, she does not just place this rage safely outside the therapeutic relationship. She understands it as something that will need to be expressed in the therapy as a significant part of the transference. In this approach, which is psychodynamic as well as feminist, transference is another key aspect. It is interesting that the only therapist who defines herself as psychodynamic is the only one who strongly identifies anger as an area to work on. The reader may ask whether this is coincidental, or whether the dynamic approach focuses more on the expression of negative feelings, and on the working through of these within the transference.

John Rowan's account demonstrates awareness of the significance of Peta's mother, and Maye Taylor echoes the importance of this relationship. She senses that woman-to-woman therapy will provide a valuable forum for working on this. Similarly, John Rowan is particularly aware of working with Peta on father issues. This raises the question of whether there is a gender-specific issue here: can women clients work best, or only work at all, with women on issues relating to their mothers, and vice versa in relation to fathers? Some therapists argue that transference transcends gender and that both parental figures can be equally dealt with by the same therapist irrespective of that therapist's gender. This is an important theme to pursue: one that is not always sufficiently discussed in the literature. It is interesting to note that in this book both John Rowan and Jennifer Mackewn discuss the probable benefits of working at some stage with another therapist of different gender to facilitate therapy moving into a new phase.

Power and empowerment are frequently mentioned in several contexts in Taylor's chapter, more so than in the other chapters, even though as she notes it is a term frequently used by Peta. Taylor expresses unease about the power connotations implied by the term 'assessment' – again this is not mentioned by the other therapists. Taylor understands assessment as lying as much with the client as the therapist. She emphasizes that it is a major decision and responsibility to take any individual into therapy. Power is looked at again as Taylor notes Peta's frequent references to the term. She discusses how she would like to have explored this further with Peta in terms of its different meanings and implications for her. It is points like this in the chapter, where the nuances of a frequently used word are examined, that Peta's comment on the detail of Taylor's approach is particularly apposite.

Empowerment of women is perhaps the underlying philosophy to this feminist approach as it is described here. Arising from this, any outcome of therapy can only be judged by Peta herself, in response to her own agenda. Taylor recognizes that Peta will not change how men are, but that she can be enabled to make some changes for herself based on a new and greater understanding. It is worth noting that in the questions to the client, Taylor is the only one who directly refers to Peta as having had a woman partner at one stage, although John Rowan does refer to this as having significance for outcome – in that she will be enabled to make a true choice of the gender of a partner. Given her presenting problem of difficulties with men, and that the information relating to the woman partner was provided in the first interview, the absence of interest on the part of the other therapists is somewhat surprising.

This approach combines psychodynamic technique, with its aware-ness of transference and unconscious processes, and a feminist philosophy. It is strikingly different from some other approaches. It actively and essentially incorporates a political understanding into working with women, encouraging them to take responsibility for what is theirs, but not to become a psychological sponge for things that are not. It recognizes that more is required for women to change their lives than individual effort. It essentially acknowledges the power of structures and the enormous influence of these, both now and in the past.

Christine Wood

As readers are now aware, Peta herself trained in art, and it therefore seemed particularly appropriate to ask an art therapist to contribute one of the approaches. Peta had previously had a very negative experience in being a student on an art therapy course, in which she found the tutor very destructive. She felt 'very damaged by her, but this one is not like that'. In fact, she was very positive about Christine Wood and her contribution. She talked at some length about her responses to this chapter, and although there is not space to record all her responses, the following captures her key feelings:

It is a very enabling text: I like her comment that I'm able to record internal dialogue. She's aware of and respectful of my struggle, and she uses and includes my own phrases; it's as if she's paying respect to my actual language. She makes very astute observations. And her picking up my insubstantial sense of self when I was growing up made a lot of sense.

Peta strongly felt that this was another therapist who was very sensitive to and responsive to her needs. Peta experienced her as being genuinely and deeply concerned for her. This clearly touched her deeply. She also appreciated that in her letter to her Chris Wood told her something about herself, which further reinforces comments made earlier in this chapter. It is interesting that she struggled with some of the art work she was asked to complete. As I noted earlier, this is very different from her experience with Jennifer Mackewn, where she was able to draw quite spontaneously. It may have been that the subject matter here was particularly difficult for her to undertake alone:

She recognizes that the pictures I made did not seem adequate to me. She really hit on something when she wondered what has happened to my use of art. She hits on something again when she remarks on my difficulty in drawing from a child's perspective – it is a kind of play. You feel light sometimes when you do it, and the lightness of that state is something I can't get into at present. So her comments are helpful and accurate although painful.

These are very valuable comments. They remind me of some of Peta's responses to John Rowan. She acknowledged that he is accurate but that she felt it too dangerous to get into. Again here she encountered a childhood experience that she sensed was significant, but she did not want to look at it. I wondered myself, as someone who knows little about art therapy, if art reaches through layers of defences quicker than verbal approaches. If that is so, those of us who do not have the knowledge base of trained art therapists need to take care. It is sometimes tempting to dabble in other approaches without always knowing the implications of so doing. It is also worth noting that on both occasions referred to here, Peta herself knew that she wished to go no further. There is a very important message coming out of this, that therapists need to listen to their clients, and to respect their own sense of what is right for them, even if therapists accurately sense where difficulties might lie.

On balance, although Peta struggled with the artistic contributions which this art therapist not unnaturally asked for, she felt very positive about the use of art in therapy, feeling that it is an effective way of accessing feelings and experiences:

I do feel that art making can be healing and helpful; and I found her comments on the pictures good – I liked them. It was particularly helpful because of my other experience with an art therapist. I sensed her really working on things with me and for me; and she had begun to do what the Gestalt therapist did, which was to engage with me. She's able to extend a hand.

As with the Gestalt therapist, Peta felt that her tendency to withdraw had been well spotted, and that this was helpful and accurate: 'She's very good, and her comments on my tendency to withdraw are absolutely right. She weaves in and out of my need to have an on-going therapeutic relationship; and that is right also'.

Christine Wood describes herself, her ideas and her training as subject to many and varied influences. What obviously stands out as different in her approach is the emphasis on art as the central means of expression. Others in this book – for example, Mackewn – may use this as an occasional tool, but Wood's is a very different perspective.

Wood notes the significance of the remarks made by Peta regarding her mother, and she comments that some feminists (and she quotes Alice Miller in support) may not take on board such issues, although, as we have seen, Taylor is also concerned to explore this area. Wood shares with Rowan an interest in Peta's life before the birth of her brother. She sent Peta a letter, which is reproduced in her chapter. She clearly wishes to make contact, and as Peta's comments indicate, she succeeds in doing so. Of all the therapists, Christine Wood is the one who was most concerned that she could not see Peta, and that Peta could not see her. Perhaps for someone so used to working with visual material, the relationship this book allowed for feels particularly strange. It does not, however, prevent her from making some valuable comments both for the reader and also for Peta.

Wood emphasizes her relationship with her client in this modality as being a three-way rather than a two-way process: the therapeutic relationship flows between the client, her art work and the therapist. This certainly adds a new dimension to the therapeutic process. The client is encouraged to develop a relationship with her own art work through which she creates what is meaningful to her. As I noted earlier, the suggestion of drawing like a child was problematic for Peta, although, as she did for John Rowan, Peta sent extra material to Christine Wood that had not been suggested or requested. This may indicate something about the client herself knowing what she wishes to communicate, and finding her own way of doing so, when she senses that her therapist is both receptive and trustworthy.

Wood also suggests the creation and maintenance of a journal as a scrapbook for Peta to record her own internal dialogue. It can contain items that were especially significant to her. I imagine this is something to be compiled by the client at home. This use of specific tasks and activities at home is again different from some other approaches. However, this may not be so different as it at first seems. Other orientations also hope that the client will carry on the therapeutic work between sessions but see this as a purely internal process. Unlike some therapists who set 'homework' tasks that often relate to external events, and which will be brought back to the session, Wood's suggestion is for a tangible means of recording the client's internal process and dialogue, as a means of helping the client really focus on what she feels.

Wood links the use of art as therapy with the Winnicottian concept of play, and sees art as a method that could usefully interrupt any impulse in Peta to withdraw. Her sessions are longer than the traditional fifty minutes, to give time to make some art work. She states the boundaries of time and place explicitly in her account, which the others do not. The reader may feel this is because these time boundaries are assumed to be in place, although there may be more variation than is evidenced here. Wood feels that clear boundaries are an important aspect of therapeutic safety. She would also (like Ormrod, another therapist who also works within the NHS) offer a time-limited contract, believing that this will assist Peta in focusing. There are considerable variations regarding contracts between the different therapists, dependent partly on the approach, partly on practicalities like client demands on the service.

We might also note the absence of some of the features noted by Maye Taylor. Like most of the therapists, Wood chooses not to identify the theme of anger. Neither does she appear to consider the significance of the gender of the therapist, to which others refer. Although it is perhaps unfair to identify Christine Wood as a feminist therapist, when she does not herself make such a claim, she does quote Alice Miller, and also one of her trainers as having 'a fierce social conscience'. In this account there is no evidence that she ascribes a role to wider society in contributing to Peta's difficulties.

Judy Moore

Peta said that because she had had some training in, and experience of, person-centred counselling, she read Judy Moore's account from a slightly different position:

I was particularly familiar with the ground on this one. It
felt comfortable and I felt she was very warm and accepting,
although she also spotted well some more difficult areas. But
the language about empathy and acceptance and congruence
were all there, and I know them. So it felt quite good,
although didn't have the impact of the decent man and the
Gestalt woman.

Whereas therapists such as John Rowan and Jennifer Mackewn
describe their training history as varied, culminating in their own
particular approach, Judy Moore does not try to integrate methods
from other approaches. Although she does not place herself at 'the
purest end of person-centred therapy', she adheres quite closely to
the person-centred tradition. In this way, her central concern is
affect, and close attention is paid to the development of empathy
and congruence. She comments that she would normally elicit information by empathic responding rather than questions, although
she notes that she *will* ask questions if appropriate. She will also
make connections for the client between different aspects of their
world. She herself says that this is again not an absolutely 'pure'
person-centred approach. It is worth commenting that within any
approach, the individuals who subscribe to it show some individual
differences (and indeed need to if they are to be themselves and not
therapeutic clones). This does not mean there are not differences
between approaches, but may mean that both between and within
approaches there is room for flexibility, as many of these therapists
have noted.

Accessing and working with feelings are therefore of prime importance to her, with the therapist paying close regard to her own
experience of being with the client. Creating a climate of trust and
acceptance is crucial in order to enable the client to discover and
encompass aspects of her self that have previously been denied
awareness. This emphasis on the client's self-discovery is significant;
person-centred therapy believes that the client, given the correct
therapeutic conditions, will find her own route to greater integration. In other words, the greatest expert on the client is the client
and not the therapist.

Judy Moore, like Maye Taylor, places considerable emphasis on
Peta's feminism and was very much in sympathy with this. She
accepts Peta's insights into her own situation, believing that many
of Peta's problems with men are inevitable in a society where 'most
men are unable to handle close relationships'. There are other ways,
too, that Judy Moore is able to feel close to Peta in her experiences
and feels that these shared features and concerns might assist the

creation of a good therapeutic alliance: their feminist understanding; also that they each have one son; and both have an interest in
spirituality. She is also able to identify the potential pitfalls of
empathic identification, recognizing the role of supervision in helping her to deal with this and other probable difficult areas.

Although there is a strong emphasis on feminism in Moore's
chapter – particularly as a significant and influential shared experience between the two women – it seems not to occupy the core of
her therapeutic stance as it does with Taylor. In Taylor's description
of therapy, there is an interweaving throughout of the political with
the personal, reflecting a belief that both are constantly and inevitably part of therapy with women. Perhaps the difference between
the two is that for Moore, although feminism is clearly deeply significant to her, it might not underpin her theory of therapy in the
same way. Instead, as we might expect in a person-centred therapist,
what underpins the therapy are core conditions, including unconditional positive regard, empathy and congruence. This is perhaps
reflected in the way the two therapists describe themselves: Maye
Taylor incorporates 'feminist' into her description of herself, while
Judy Moore does not.

There is an interesting dilemma which Judy Moore alludes to,
which may help explain the different way in which these two feminists incorporate and understand feminism in the context of
therapeutic practice. Taylor comments that feminism is not an easy
option; that it is not without its own difficulties. Moore takes up
this same theme but with a different emphasis. She recognizes that
the conceptual understanding of a woman's difficulties arising from
feminism are enlightening and helpful. But she sees disadvantages
too. Because the person-centred approach places such emphasis on
feelings, intellectual understanding can impede that process. The
person-centred approach is concerned with the recognition, validation
and direct experience of these feelings, and too great an emphasis
on understanding the political dimension can become a way of
defending against them. A careful balance has to be achieved so that
intellectual process and consequent understanding are not invali-
dated, but neither are feelings blocked.

An interesting comparison can be made between the person-centred
approach, with its emphasis on the necessity of the therapist providing core conditions, and the cognitive-behavioural model described
by Ormrod, with its emphasis on identifying and understanding the
core beliefs of the client. Again, there is potentially a wide divergence
between concentrating in therapy on an individual's core beliefs
that affect her thinking and behaviour (Ormrod), and taking into
account the core beliefs of a society which affect the thinking and

behaviour of many members of a society (feminist therapists). We may well begin to feel, as we examine the basic assumptions and beliefs of these different approaches, that they should be placed at very different places on the therapeutic continuum.

Moore's allusions to feminism were important to Peta, although she recognized a different emphasis in her approach from Maye Taylor's:

> I did really like the way she acknowledged that it mattered to me and to her. And I liked knowing that she had a son too. It does help to know about the person, and they're prepared to share things with you. It makes me feel more equal and closer to the person. And all the feminists did that, although they were quite different in other ways.

As has been noted previously Peta found it helpful to know something about the therapist, but her comments here about experiencing this as helping to equalize the relationship are significant. Judy Moore sees the equalizing of power as a central tenet in the person-centred approach; and that remaining both empathic and accepting is essential to achieving that end. It is an aspect of therapy that is explored and acknowledged in different ways by several of the other therapists. Readers may wish to consider for themselves how power is perceived and responded to by different models of therapy. A question that could be posed is whether some approaches are more aware than others of this issue.

In one sense, the past does not figure very largely in Judy Moore's account, in that in terms of the actual process of working there is an emphasis on the therapist working with the here-and-now relationship with her client. However, in another sense, the past is clearly seen as relevant and Moore's questions relate to past events: she is the only one to ask about Peta's marriage, and she goes on to enquire into the patterns in her relationships. It is interesting that only she and John Ormrod specifically ask about the bullying at school, although nowadays there is an awareness of the long-term effects of this. Moore also recognizes how some patterns in Peta's childhood have repeated into adulthood. The past as being influential over Peta's present is thus recognized, but the focus of the work is decided and led by the client through the present relationship with her therapist.

In Moore's chapter, there are many terms that are not found elsewhere and that are distinctive to this approach. Transference as a concept, although frequently alluded to in other accounts, is noticeable by its absence. 'The actualizing tendency' – the drive of the healthiest part of the person towards becoming an integrated whole

– is discussed, and the concept of incongruence between different parts of the self is stressed. The description at the end of her chapter of a 'fully functioning person', resonates somewhat with the description of Rowan's 'real self', although the methods of achieving these desired states are extremely different in the two models. The different styles of contracts for clients have been mentioned in relation to other therapeutic models. An essential element of the person-centred approach is perhaps reflected in its stance on contracts. The therapist indicates that she is prepared to be flexible on both frequency and duration of sessions and that the client comes 'for as long as it seems helpful to her'. In this way, the client determines the ending in the same way as she has determined the therapy.

Summary

Writing this last chapter has proved to be a task that has been stimulating and challenging while also being somewhat daunting. So much can be said about these contributions and yet they speak for themselves. In my attempt to give an overview of the work of the six therapists, I am aware that much more of interest and relevance can be said and asked. My hope is that readers will use these chapters to inform their own thinking, to ask the questions and to make the comments that I have not included here.

An essential element of this chapter has been integrating the responses of Peta herself into my own comments on the six therapists. I hope I have given her and all the therapists a sense of the valuable and unique contribution they have all made. All those involved have been willing to put themselves on the line: Peta by sharing herself with us so honestly and openly, and the therapists by allowing us to see how they think and work.

Therapists have sometimes been criticized for not being prepared to move from the shelter and privacy of the consulting room into the scrutiny of the wider world. Certainly, this is not the case for the therapists who have written here. Their ability and willingness to explain their methods and ideas in the context of a real person's story is indeed commendable. All those who participated commented on the limitations of a project of this kind. These do, of course, exist – as is the case with any exploration of this nature. However, limitations in part do not invalidate the whole, and it is hoped that this book, together with others in the series, will prove a stimulating source of discussion and enquiry.

In our last meeting together, as Peta and I were discussing this last chapter, we wondered how to conclude it. We both felt that the reader may wonder what happened next, particularly in view of the difficulties we had encountered during this latter stage, which I have described at the beginning of this chapter. It seemed therefore to be a fitting end to agree that I would inform the reader that I did arrange for Peta to enter therapy, and when I last met her she was anticipating this eagerly. She wanted the reader to know that she was seeing a male therapist, considerably older than herself. Peta described herself as 'currently surrounded by women' (she now has a loving relationship with a woman partner), and she was looking forward to working with an older man, commenting that she had very little experience of that type of relationship. She was wondering how all the father material would emerge and be dealt with. And her last comment to me was, 'I hope he's good at working with transference!'

NATIONAL UNIVERSITY
LIBRARY   SAN DIEGO